DYSLEXIA 101
Truths, Myths and What ***Really*** Works

By Marianne Sunderland

To my husband, Laurence, for your unending support and for helping me to understand what it is like to be dyslexic. You are amazing!

To my kids, Zac, Abby, Toby, Jessie, Lydia, Katherine, Ben and Paul-Louis.
Thank you for being patient with me while I learned about dyslexia and for your support during the writing of this book.

TABLE OF CONTENTS

APPENDIXES

INTRODUCTION

According to the National Institutes of Health (NIH), 17% of our nation's children have trouble learning to read. More than 2.9 million school-age children in the United States – approximately six percent of the student population – are diagnosed with learning disabilities. When we first realized that our otherwise bright oldest child was not learning to read as he should, we began looking for answers. That was 17 years ago. He learned to read, graduated from high school with honors, and has gone on to do amazing things with his life. Our journey to discover what held him back in reading and how to help him had a steep learning curve. Since then, we have 7 more children – 6 who have struggled in some way to learn to read

Researchers estimate that learning to read, will be the hardest thing that approximately 20% of the general population will ever do. Interestingly, dyslexics make up a disproportionately large number of our world's entrepreneurs. Julie Logan of the Cass Business School in London found that 35% of the entrepreneurs that she interviewed identified themselves as dyslexic. This makes sense as more and more successful business people have begun to step up and talk about their experiences with dyslexia - Richard Branson of the Virgin Empire, Charles Schwab, the founder of the discount brokerage that bears his name, John Chambers, chief executive of Cisco, Craig McGraw, the cellular phone pioneer, and Paul Orfalea, founder of the Kinko's copy chain to name just a few.

On the other end of the spectrum, researchers at the University of Texas Medical Branch in conjunction with the Texas Department of Criminal Justice (published 2000) have found that dyslexics make up 48% of prison inmates - a disproportionately high number. What do these statistics tell us about the nature of dyslexia? Illiteracy is tied to a disappointing variety of social ills. The way that dyslexia is handled in the early years has a significant impact on the future success or failure of the dyslexic learner.

Unfortunately, there is a lack of understanding of what causes these difficulties in learning to read despite the fact that there is a growing body of scientifically-based research on what dyslexia is and how to effectively teach dyslexics to read, write and spell. Unsuspecting parents go through everything from frustration to fear, and far too often, helplessness, in their quest to help their child.

Writing about dyslexia is a passion of mine because of our own experience raising and teaching our kids with dyslexia. I know how it feels to be utterly confused by an otherwise bright child who just doesn't 'get' reading. I know how overwhelming it was to search through web site after web site, book after book, searching for the answers. I know how many false starts and disappointments we went through before we found what really works. I saw how being unable to read and write well affected my kids as they grew up. How I wish I could go back, knowing what I know now and do things differently.

Over the years I have come to learn that our experience is far from exceptional. In fact, many parents of struggling readers waste untold amounts of time and energy because of misinformation and their own limited understanding of dyslexia. This experience has been the impetus for this book – *to encourage other parents that, with the correct information and the right methods, their children can not only learn to read and spell and write, but to understand the inherent strengths of the dyslexic mind, embrace them and find success.*

Our perseverance paid off and after years of sifting through the research and writings of experts, trying some of this and some of that, we began to understand more fully the typical signs of dyslexia, how to test for dyslexia and how to effectively help our kids not only succeed but to thrive. Understanding dyslexia can be complicated, but *Dyslexia 101* will attempt to provide the information you need, exposing the myths and defining the truths, so that you can help your child succeed.

From research to real life, prevention to remediation, preschool to college and from the practical to the spiritual, *Dyslexia 101* will walk you through figuring out your child's reading struggles and give you the information you need to help them to succeed.

Because the scope and study of dyslexia is constantly expanding, adding new information to our understanding of dyslexia, the appendixes in the back of the book are full of resources and links to help you as your further your own understanding of the intricacies of the dyslexic mind.

Chapter 1: What is Dyslexia?

Before the National Institutes of Health began their research in the 1980's, the definition of dyslexia was limited by our lack of understanding. If a child was otherwise bright, had no vision or hearing problems, but struggled learning to read, he or she was considered dyslexic. No one knew why or what to do about it.

In 2000, Sally Shaywitz, author of *Overcoming Dyslexia*, and researcher at Yale University, looked closer at the brains of good readers and poor readers. She and her team used Functional MRIs to look at the neural pathways that were used during reading by both 'good' readers and poor readers. What they saw drastically enhanced what professionals know about the mechanics behind dyslexia. The researchers were amazed to see that the pathways of the good readers were direct: impulses transferred directly from the eyes to the reading center of the brain; while the poor readers' pathway was much more convoluted.

Defining Dyslexia

More is known about dyslexia now than ever before. We now know that it is a biological condition, genetically based, that results in structural differences in the brain. These differences can affect:

• short term memory
• visual and auditory information processing
• phonological processing, especially in hearing the smallest sounds in words
• speed of processing information
• organization and sequencing

Dyslexia is complex. A dyslexic can struggle because of slow auditory and visual processing, weak short term memory or all of these and in varying degrees. This processing glitch manifests in numerous ways within the classroom environment or business place. A dyslexic may have slow, inaccurate reading, terrible spelling, a difficulty with penmanship (also known as dysgraphia) or a variety of other struggles. The basic issue in the early stages of dyslexia is with reading and spelling.

However, dyslexic people may also have trouble speaking clearly, pronouncing new or long words, or learning a foreign language. For this reason, dyslexia cannot be neatly categorized. Generally stated, **dyslexia is an inherited condition, neurologically-based, that causes interference with the processing of language.**

Statistics show that:
- 5% of kids will learn to read on their own
- 20-30% will learn to read relatively easily once exposed to formal instruction; most methods will be effective
- 30-50% will find learning to read to be difficult without direct systematic, explicit instruction
- 30-50% will find learning to read to be the most difficult challenge they will ever face
- 50-60% of kids with dyslexia have ADD or ADHD

Despite these statistics, please know that **ALL CHILDREN CAN BE TAUGHT TO READ**.

What Dyslexia Isn't: Myths and Facts

Because dyslexia has been misunderstood for so long, there are a lot of misperceptions about what dyslexia is and is not. Scientific research on how the brain works has shed light on a lot of these myths. Here are 10 of the most common myths {and truths} about dyslexia.

Myth: Dyslexia doesn't exist.

Fact: Dyslexia is one of the most researched and documented conditions that impacts children. Dyslexia is genetically based and has been shown to be clearly related to neurophysiological differences in brain function.

Myth: Learning disabilities are correlated to IQ.

Fact: Dyslexia is not related to intelligence. In fact, one of the clear signs that a child may have dyslexia is that there is a discrepancy between their intelligence (average to above-average) and their processing speeds and academic performance. Dyslexics are intelligent and lean towards creative strengths such as art, music, athletics, mechanical skills, people skills, 3D visual-spatial skills, intuition

14

and global thinking (being able to see the big picture). Click here to read a list of over 200 'famous' dyslexics that have accomplished great things, not despite their dyslexia but because of their dyslexic gifts.

Myth: Children will outgrow dyslexia.
Fact: Research shows that if a child is struggling with reading, writing and spelling in mid-first grade, there is a 90% chance that the child will still be struggling in 8th grade and into adulthood. Knowing this, waiting for your child to improve is not a good option. In my experience, kids just get further and further behind, lose confidence and feel frustrated. It takes less time to fix reading and spelling difficulties when dyslexia is discovered and treated early. However, it is never too late.

Myth: Dyslexia is caused by bad diet, bad parenting or watching too much TV.
Fact: Dyslexia is genetically based. Although bad diet, bad parenting and watching too much TV aren't good for any child and certainly won't help the situation.

Myth: Dyslexia can be helped with medication.

Fact: There is no medication to help with dyslexia. However, as many as 60% of kids with dyslexia also have Attention Deficit Disorder {ADD}. There are some medications for ADD, but they won't help with reading, writing and spelling – only attention issues.

Myth: Dyslexia is a visual problem.

Fact: Most kids reverse letters or numbers while they are learning. Continued reversals after 2 years of instruction is considered a sign of dyslexia. This, however, is not a vision issue. Dyslexia is a language processing disorder – difficulty relating sounds to symbols.

Myth: Dyslexia affects more boys than girls.

Fact: More boys are sent in for dyslexia testing than girls, but research shows that an equal amount of boys and girls are affected by dyslexia. Because boys tend to act out their frustrations of not doing well in class, they are noticed and sent in for testing. Girls who aren't doing well in class tend to be more quiet

16

and try to avoid being noticed. Sometimes they are only diagnosed in high school or college.

Myth: Dyslexics are just lazy and need to work harder.

Fact: Research has shown by the use of functional MRIs and brain mapping that slower readers use different parts of their brains when reading and working with language. The findings provide evidence that people with dyslexia are not poorly taught, lazy, or stupid but have an inborn brain abnormality that has nothing to do with intelligence.

Myth: Accommodations (more time for tests, not counting spelling, having a notetaker)for kids with dyslexia are a crutch.

Fact: Dyslexics are just as intelligent as their peers but may need more time on tests to be able to reflect what they really know. The difficulties in taking notes is so profound that students will often miss the entire meaning of a lecture just trying to copy down the pertinent words.

Myth: Dyslexia is untreatable.

Fact: There are successful treatments for dyslexia. It is not a disease that can be treated with a pill. It is a way of thinking, the way the brain is wired and how it processes information. Research has shown that the brain can actually be rewired if the individual is taught with systematic, explicit, sequential phonics taught in a multi-sensory way.

These myths are responsible for much misunderstanding among everyone from family members and friends to teachers and administrators in the school house. It is vitally important that the correct information is understood so that dyslexics can get the help they need without delay and so that they can understand that though reading, writing and spelling are harder for them to master, they possess many other gifts and talents that can more than make up for these losses.

Chapter 2: How to Know if You or Your Child is Dyslexic

Despite the fact that we were a reading family that spent many hours reading to and conversing with our oldest child, he was still struggling to 'crack the code' of reading at 7 years old. It was as if everything we had taught him the previous day had mysteriously leaked out sometime in the night so that our reading lessons seldom progressed past some of the most basic of phonics rules. We were encouraged by well-meaning people to wait, that he was probably a 'late bloomer'. "Some kids just catch on later." "He is a boy you know!" I suppose that there was something in this advice that was reassuring. Believing that his struggles in learning to read were developmentally-based meant that his struggles were not my fault and that there was nothing that could be done but wait. What we didn't know then is that there are many measurable signs that a person may have dyslexia and our son had quite a few of them.

The truth is that although a small number of reading struggles may be due to a developmental lag, many are not. There **are** ways to detect serious potential reading difficulties and effective interventions that can be implemented even **before** first grade. In fact, early screening is vitally important in preventing a child from falling behind. Discovering dyslexia early and intervening with research-based treatments can result in your struggling reader developing confidence, enjoying reading, reading more and reading better. The longer you wait to intervene means more hours of intervention to have your child catch up, an increased chance that your child will never catch up, greater risk of loss of self-esteem, and the likelihood that your child will miss out on the majority of the reading content and vocabulary growth of his or her peers.

If you are reading this and your child is older, maybe even it is you or another adult you know that has dyslexia - know that it is **never too late**. Our oldest son, the 'late bloomer', did learn to read despite our lack of understanding and intervention at an early age. It wasn't until he was 12 years old that he would pick up a book and read it on his own for pleasure. We laid a foundation for him of listening to good literature, modified his school work in our homeschool and persevered with reading practice week after week. He still struggles with spelling, as do many adult dyslexics, but has found a career path that he loves and has gone on to do great things. See chapter Appendix C for more of our family's dyslexia story.

Signs of Dyslexia

You may be wondering if you or one of your family members have dyslexia. There are signs and characteristics that parents and teachers can look for. If your child has 3 or more symptoms and there is a family history of dyslexia, you should consider having your child tested when they turn five.

In Preschool:
- delayed speech
- mixing up sounds and syllables in long words
- stuttering
- left-right confusion
- trouble rhyming

- trouble memorizing their address, phone number or the alphabet
- trouble learning to tie shoes

In Elementary School:
- does not enjoy reading but likes being read to
- slow, inaccurate reading
- uses context clues rather than sounding words out
- skips or misreads little words (at, to, of)
- poor spelling - very phonetic
- trouble telling time on a clock with hands
- difficulty expressing self
- inattentiveness, distractibility
- slow and messy handwriting - also called dysgraphia
- letter and number reversals after first grade
- trouble memorizing math facts
- hesitant speech; difficulty finding the right words to express self
- extremely messy bedroom, backpack or desk
- dreads going to school

Adolescence and Adulthood:

All of the above signs plus:

- difficulty processing auditory information
- losing possessions; poor organizational skills
- slow reading; low comprehension
- difficulty remembering the names of people and places
- difficulty organizing ideas to write a paper
- difficulty reading music
- unable to master a foreign language
- inability to recall numbers in proper sequence
- lowered self-esteem due to past frustrations and failures
- may drop out of high school

Most non-dyslexic kids need 3-4 years of instruction to become proficient readers. The key to knowing whether your child's lack of progress in reading is outside the range of normal, and may be a learning disability like dyslexia, is to note if there are enough warning signs and a lack of any significant improvement. While no two people with dyslexia are exactly the same, if someone struggles with spelling, is a slow reader and has 3 or more of these classic signs, it would be a good idea to get that person tested for dyslexia. I will talk more on testing in the next chapter.

Benchmarks of Reading

Benchmarks of reading are another way to assess your child's fluency with the printed word based on age. This list from the National Academy of Sciences article titled, *Preventing Reading Difficulties in Young Children* details the benchmark reading accomplishments that a child should have mastered by the end of Kindergarten:

- Knows the parts of a book and their functions.
- Begins to track print when listening to a familiar text being read or when rereading own writing.
- "Reads" familiar texts emergently, i.e., not necessarily verbatim from the print alone.
- Recognizes and can name all uppercase and lowercase letters.
- Understands that the sequence of letters in a written word represents the sequence of sounds

(phonemes) in a spoken word (alphabetic principle).

- Learns many, though not all, one-to-one letter-sound correspondences.
- Recognizes some words by sight, including a few very common ones (a, the, I, my, you, is, are).
- Uses new vocabulary and grammatical constructions in own speech.
- Makes appropriate switches from oral to written language situations.
- Notices when simple sentences fail to make sense.
- Connects information and events in texts to life, and life to text experiences.
- Retells, reenacts, or dramatizes stories or parts of stories.
- Listens attentively to books teacher reads to class.
- Can name some book titles and authors.
- Demonstrates familiarity with a number of types or genres of text (e.g., storybooks, expository texts, poems, newspapers, and everyday print such as signs, notices, labels).
- Correctly answers questions about stories read aloud.

- Makes predictions based on illustrations or portions of stories.
- Demonstrates understanding that spoken words consist of a sequence of phonemes.
- Given spoken sets like "dan, dan, den," can identify the first two as being the same and the third as different.
- Given spoken sets like "dak, pat, zen," can identify the first two as sharing a same sound.
- Given spoken segments, can merge them into a meaningful target word.
- Given a spoken word, can produce another word that rhymes with it.
- Independently writes many uppercase and lowercase letters.
- Uses phonemic awareness and letter knowledge to spell independently (invented or creative spelling).
- Writes (unconventionally) to express own meaning.
- Builds a repertoire of some conventionally spelled words.
- Shows awareness of distinction between "kid writing" and conventional orthography.
- Writes own name (first and last) and the first names of some friends or classmates.

• Can write most letters and some words when they
  are dictated.

You can find more benchmarks of reading at National
Academy of Sciences web site at
http://www.nap.edu/read/6023/chapter/1.

If you suspect that your child may have an underlying
problem causing his or her learning struggles, you
may want to consider having them tested. Because
dyslexia is a widely varying problem with a variety of
factors at play causing problems, it is important to
find a qualified tester who is experienced with
reading and is knowledgable about dyslexia. The
next chapter will tell more about the testing process,
how to find a tester in your area, and how to know if
an educational tester is the right one to test your
child.

Chapter 3: When to Get Testing

When our son was 7 1/2, he still had made little progress with his reading. He struggled to remember vowel sounds, he reversed small words like *was* and *saw*, his reading was choppy and though he had just seen a word in one sentence, he could not recognize it in the following sentence. He was such a bright and precocious child, my husband and I just knew that something wasn't right. We asked around and discovered that there was an educational tester at the local Christian school that would test him. The testing he received, revealed that he indeed was a smart little boy but that his visual and auditory processing was slow and his short term memory was weak. Although learning that he had dyslexia was disappointing in some regards, it was a relief to know what was causing his struggles and to learn some ways to help him more effectively.

Types of Testing

There are different types of testing, depending on the goal. Having your child tested by the public school is different than hiring a private tester and will be covered more fully in Chapter 5: Navigating the Public School System.

Quick Assessment: The least expensive and least time consuming type of testing is done by an educational therapist (tutor) who specializes in reading. This type of assessment will help you know what specific instructional needs your child needs to get caught up or on track with schoolwork.

Limited Testing of Specific Language Areas: This middle level of assessment can be done at a specialized reading clinic and does not include in-depth IQ and neuropsychological testing. Please note that this type of reading clinic is one that specializes in dyslexia, not the Sylvan or Kumon general tutoring centers. For example, Lindamood-Bell centers can evaluate oral language skills, word attack and comprehension skills. They can also test for auditory processing issues.

Full Psycho-educational Testing: Includes a battery of standardized tests as well as some non standardized assessments specifically chosen by the licensed tester to evaluate the specific issues of each individual. Includes a detailed questionnaire about the history of your child's development and behavior. This also includes IQ testing to compare your child's potential to performance. A significant difference between these two areas is considered one of the hallmark signs of dyslexia. This is the only type of testing that will result in an official diagnosis of dyslexia.

Frequently Asked Questions About Testing for Dyslexia

Why Test for Dyslexia?

If you suspect that your child has dyslexia because of his or her struggles with reading and spelling or the number of typical signs of dyslexia they have, do you need to have them tested? It depends. Even though dyslexia is the most common reason for an otherwise bright person to struggle with reading, accurate testing can help you know their particular weaknesses and the best way to tutor them. Testing and receiving a diagnosis can be helpful to qualify for receiving services in schools and colleges. If your child is enrolled in the public school and you are seeking testing and tutoring there, the process will be a bit different. Chapter 5 on Navigating the Public School System will outline in detail the process for obtaining testing and tutoring there.

Which tests are given?

The standardized tests that kids take each year in school are academic tests and measure how much they know in each subject – math, history, science, etc. The type of test for dyslexia is a diagnostic test. The administration of an appropriate diagnostic test can show in which specific areas your child is weak. These results can be used to better understand areas to focus on in school or therapy and also prove eligibility for special programs in schools and colleges.

There is not one specific test for dyslexia. A diagnosis is obtained by piecing together information from different subtests of standardized tests along with information gathered from less formal assessments. This is why it is so important to find an experienced and knowledgeable tester that is familiar with dyslexia so that the testing is accurate and useful. A series of tests (or a sub-series of tests) are usually chosen based on the issues that the child is having. Areas tested include: IQ, language abilities, academic achievement in specific areas, expressive oral language, expressive written language, receptive oral language, receptive written language, intellectual functioning, cognitive processing, and educational achievement. The reason that an IQ test is administered is to determine if there is a gap between what your child is capable of and what he is actually achieving. This is a tell-tale sign of dyslexia. This will help to determine whether the learning problems are specific to reading or if they are related to something else such as ADD/ADHD, emotional disorders, or physical or sensory problems.

Area Tested	Type of Skill Tested	Possible Test Used
Reading Words	Letter and Word Decoding	- Woodcock Reading Mastery Test - Woodcock-Johnson Psychological Battery - Weschsler Individual Achievement Test - The Decoding Skills Test - The Kaufman Test of Educational Achievement
Pre-Reading Skills	Phonemic Awareness	- Lindamood Auditory Conceptualization Test - Rosner Test of Auditory Analysis Skills - Torgesen-Bryant Test of Phonological Awareness (TOPA) - Test of Phonological Skills (Linguisystems) - Yopp-Singer Sound Blending Test
	Alphabet Knowledge	- Slingerland Screening Test - Emergent Literacy Survey - Woodcock Reading Mastery Test

Area Tested	Type of Skill Tested	Possible Test Used
Reading Fluency & Comprehension	Oral Reading	- Gray Oral Reading Test - Informal Reading Inventory
	Silent Reading Comprehen-sion	- Woodcock-Johnson - Nelson-Denny - Weschsler Individual Achievement Test - Kaufman Test of Educational Achievement
Spelling	Writing Words from Dictation	- Test of Written Language - Rapid Automatic Naming - Weschsler Individual Achievement Test
Oral Language Skills	Listening Comprehension	- Test of Language Development - Rapid Automatic Naming - Clinical Evaluation of Language Fundamentals

Area Tested	Type of Skill Tested	Possible Test Used
	Expressive Language	- Test of Written Language - Rapid Automatic Naming - Weschsler Individual Achievement Test
Writing	Composing a Story	- Test of Written Language - Weschsler Individual Achievement Test
	Knowledge of Symbolic Conventions	- Test of Written Language - Test of Written Expression - Woodcock-Johnson
Intellectual Ability	Verbal Reasoning	- Weschsler Intelligence Scale for Children - III - Test of Nonverbal Intelligence - Woodcock-Johnson Test of Cognitive Abilities
Visual-Motor Skills	Form Copying	- Bender Gestalt Test - Visual Motor Integration Test
	Writing	- Rex Complex Figure Drawing - Slingerland Screening Test

Who gives the tests?

It is important that the professional who tests your child be an expert in dyslexia so that they understand which tests to give and how to score them. A person who is qualified to test a child with reading difficulties must have a strong background in language, reading, writing and psychological evaluation. Their training will usually be in psychology, reading and language education, or speech/language pathology.

How to determine if a tester is qualified

If you decide to have your child privately tested, there are some questions to ask to help you identify a good evaluator.

Questions to ask a potential tester:
- What is your training?
- What license do you hold?
- How long have you been evaluating children?
- Are you familiar with dyslexia? What do you think dyslexia is?
- What are some of the tests that you use?

- Will you be able to refer us to an educational therapist?
- Will you meet with us and provide a written report after the testing?
- If my child his diagnosed with dyslexia, what specific method would you recommend?

How to find a dyslexia tester in your area

It may be difficult to find a tester in your area. You may have to drive some ways to find someone who is uniquely qualified. To find a tester in your area contact one of the following organizations:

International Dyslexia Association   http://eida.org
Academic Language Therapy Association   http://www.altaread.org
Association of Educational Therapists   http://www.aetonline.org

What age should be tested?

People can be tested for dyslexia from about age 5. Since early intervention has been shown to decrease any lag in education, the earlier the better.

Can the public school give the tests?

Public schools are required to test children who live in their service area, whether they attend the school or not. However, most public schools do not test for dyslexia. They are testing children to see if they are eligible for special education services. There is a big difference between eligibility testing and diagnostic testing. Often times, the school district testers are not even aware that there are tests for dyslexia that can be administered. If you speak to the school, be sure to ask the questions above to determine if they meet the qualifications and that they can provide the right type of information that you are looking for – specifically if your child has dyslexia and what his or her specific areas of weakness are.

How much does it cost?

The cost of testing varies from state to state. In Southern California where we live, it can cost between three hundred dollars and several thousand dollars. Dyslexia is not considered a medical condition so it is not covered by insurance.

A few last tips for testing

- Select an evaluator that is especially knowledgeable in the specific area that you have concerns. Some specialize in ADD/ADHD while others are more knowledgeable about reading, math, or writing.
- Keep notes of which specific areas your child is struggling so that the tester knows better what to test for.
- Testing your child is not always necessary for teaching them successfully. Know that regardless of teaching methods, teaching reading and other language arts to a dyslexic child takes more time, more intensity and much more practice than teaching a child without dyslexia.

Chapter 4: Reading Instruction That Works

Getting informed is paramount for parents to be the best advocates for their dyslexic children. Knowing what dyslexia is and is not, and how and when to get testing will help you and your child to understand best what your child needs to succeed. Indeed, these things are important to know, but the million dollar question remains, "How do you get them reading?"

Dyslexic learners can all learn to read. It takes time, diligence and the **right methods**. While some children will learn to read fairly easily with any method, dyslexic learners need to be systematically and explicitly taught and retaught every aspect of reading. It simply does not come naturally and needs to be taught, every step of the way.

The International Dyslexia Association publishes a booklet about the **best instruction methods** for children with dyslexia. They are based on the latest research as well as the consensus of thousands of educational therapists over 50 years. We'll look at what the experts say about **what** to teach and **how** to teach along with the impact of individual learning styles and then we'll look at some programs that can be used at home that follow these guidelines.

What to Teach

Phonemic Awareness: How to listen to a single word or syllable and break it into its individual sounds. Students should be able to change sounds, remove sounds and compare sounds all in their head. Research has shown that an early deficit in this area is a sure sign of reading problems in the future.

Sounds-Symbol Association: The knowledge of the various sounds in our language and their corresponding letter or combination of letters that represent those sounds. This includes blending sounds together into words and segmenting or taking whole words apart into individual sounds.

Syllabication Instruction: Instruction of the six basic syllable types and how these formations affect the composite letters' sounds.

Morphology: The study of base words, roots, prefixes and suffixes.

Semantics: Instruction in reading comprehension strategies.

How to Teach

Most anything you will read about effective reading instruction now a days will talk about research-based instruction methods or the Orton-Gillingham method. The basic multi-sensory structured language technique known as the Orton-Gillingham approach was developed in the 1930s and 1940s. During the 1920s a neurologist named Samuel Orton began an intensive study of a group of people whom he called 'word blind'. After studying what they could and couldn't do, he took an interest in learning whether or not these children could learn to read. For many years he worked with Anna Gillingham and a team of others and eventually came up with an approach to teaching reading that taught the structure of sound-symbol relationships and used all of the senses to reinforce these associations. Since then, the Orton-Gillingham approach has been adapted and modified by institutions, agencies and private educational therapists. Here are the individual facets of an effective reading program.

Simultaneous & Multi-Sensory: Research has shown that dyslexics using all of their senses as they learn (visual, auditory, tactile and kinesthetic) are better able to store and retrieve information. Using as many of the senses as possible at once (simultaneously) is best.

Systematic and Cumulative: Multi-sensory language instruction requires that the organization of material follows the logical order of the language. The sequence must begin with the easiest and most basic elements and progress methodically to more difficult concepts. Material must be taught systematically to strengthen memory. Introduce a rule, practice until is is mastered, and do lots of review.

Direct instruction: Dyslexic learners do not naturally pick up the rules of written language. Some of you are rolling on the floor laughing right now because this may seem like the understatement of the year! Every rule must be taught directly and practiced until mastered.

Diagnostic Teaching: Teaching must be individualized and the student's needs and progress must be constantly reassessed.

Synthetic and Analytic Instruction: Multi-sensory, structured language programs should include both synthetic and analytic instruction. Synthetic instruction presents the parts of the language and then teaches how the parts work together to form a whole. Analytic instruction presents the whole and teaches how this can be broken down into its component parts.

The end of this chapter will list some of the best, research-based programs designed for parents to tutor their own children at home. These are appropriate for the homeschooled child as much as the public or private-schooled child.

Understanding Learning Styles

Learning style is a broad term used to describe the factors that influence **all aspects** of learning - dyslexic or not. You may have heard the common, simplified view of learning styles as a preference of either the auditory, visual or kinesthetic pathway. While all people use every one of these pathways for learning; most people prefer one over the other. There are many factors that affect a person's ability to learn.

One of the most widely used and researched models of learning styles is the Dunn and Dunn model which is outlined by the following areas of individual preference:

Environmental

How is your child affected by:
• sound
• light
• temperature

• design

Is your child effected by noise or bright lights? Do they struggle with a cluttered work space?

Emotional

What is your child's level of:

• motivation

• persistence

• responsibility

• need for structure

Does your child lack confidence or get overwhelmed by big projects? Do they thrive with a loose schedule or do they need instruction every minute?

Sociological

What are your child's needs for interaction:

• learning by self

• pairs

• peers

• with an adult

Does your child like working with others, by himself or does he need you right next to him?

Physiological

What are your child's particular physical needs:

• perceptual preference (auditory, visual, kinesthetic)

• food and drink intake

• effect of time of day on ability to study

• level of mobility allowed

Does your child learn better by hearing, seeing, or by getting her hands on things? Do they learn better in the morning or in the afternoon? Does your child need to move around and stretch frequently?

Psychological

• global or analytical preferences

• impulsive or reflective

Does your child need to learn the big picture first? Does your child need time for quiet reflection?

Understanding your child's learning style, and helping him or her to understand it will help in creating, or seeking, an atmosphere that is the most conducive to learning.

While the length of this list this might make this seem overwhelming at first, it really is fairly intuitive. By intentionally observing your children everyday with these factors in mind, you will come to know what triggers struggles for your child. I have one daughter who simply cannot focus if there is a lot of noise in the room. I have another daughter who likes to listen to music while she does her schoolwork. Evaluating this in your children isn't done overnight. Adjusting your home to create a more effective learning environment can be done incrementally and perfected over time.

'Typical' Learning Styles of Dyslexics
As many as 80% of struggling learners are right-brain dominant. Not that right-brain dominance is a weakness. Considering that most school curriculums teach in a more left-brained style sheds light on a dyslexic's school day struggles. Look at the following chart of right and left-brain functions and then think about what environment a dyslexic student would most thrive in.

Left Brain Functions	Right Brain Functions
uses logic	uses feeling
detail oriented	"big picture" oriented
verbal	non verbal
facts rule	imagination rules
words & language	symbols & images
math & science	philosophy & religion
order/pattern perception	spatial perception
knows object name	knows object function
reality based	fantasy based
forms strategies	presents possibilities
practical	impetuous
safe	risk taking

The typical public or private school classroom uses textbooks, workbooks, worksheets, rote memorization, timed tests, and lectures. If your child is struggling with these methods of schooling, there are accommodations available to help them in the classroom environment. Teachers may do well to change some of the ways they are teaching to tap into the strong right-brain strengths – music, color, emotion, humor. By doing this teachers are in a sense, speaking their language. For more on teaching strategies for the classroom, please refer to Chapter 18: A Note for Teachers.

Research-Based Reading Programs to Use at Home

"There are no universally effective programs, but there are knowledgable principles that need to be incorporated in all programs about how we teach written language."
Dr. Maryanne Wolf

There are many reading programs available to help struggling readers. Reading programs should include the research-based elements presented earlier in the chapter, addressing the specific needs of each child. Effective programs present information in a way that is the most beneficial to the child's learning style. In the past few years, there has been an explosion of dyslexia treatment programs.

The following programs are ones that can be used at home while homeschooling or if you choose to augment your child's program at the public or private school. Remember that no one program will be exactly what you need to teach your child all he or she needs to know. Adapting any curriculum to meet the particular learning style of your child and adding more practice where needed are two ways to individualize any curriculum to your unique child.

At-Home Reading Curriculums for Dyslexia

Reading Horizons

Reading Horizons has been round since 1984 designing research-based literacy instruction for the public schools. Recently, they developed two online, computer programs that can be done from home; one for younger kids called Discovery at Home and one for the older struggling reader called v5. This program contains all of the standards of the International Dyslexia Association. The people behind the company are experienced educational experts with first-hand experience working with kids with dyslexia. The customer support is excellent and their web site is a wealth of the kids of information on how to effectively teach kids with dyslexia. At first it may seem somewhat expensive ($199 for one year), compared to weekly tutoring, both financially and in time out of the home, Reading Horizons is a great, efficient and inexpensive way to teach reading, spelling and reading comprehension. One yearly membership is good for up to two students.

All About Reading

Now **this** is a fun program! While Reading Horizons is intense phonics instruction with practice geared for the older struggling reader, All About Reading is hands on, simultaneously multi-sensory introduction into the written word. Every lesson comes with an engaging phonemic awareness activity that is so fun, my son doesn't know he is learning one of the most foundational skills of reading success. Lessons are completely scripted so there is little prep time for mom. The customer service at All About Learning Press is top notch. Specifically designed for the homeschooled student that struggles with reading. All About Reading includes decoding skills, fluency, comprehension, vocabulary, and lots of reading practice. Comes with a one-year 100% money back guarantee if you are not satisfied.

Lexercise

Lexercise is another online dyslexia program. Students meet with their online tutor each week and complete assignments, including an impressive array of games, at home. Lexercise and their 'clinicians' follow an Orton-Gillingham approach.

Barton Reading and Spelling Method

A program specifically designed for parents of dyslexic children. Completely scripted with very detailed, research-based activities. In 10 levels, this program can be done at home by the parent or a local tutor can be hired. We have used this program both at home and with an outside tutor. It does work, however, in our experience with a profoundly dyslexic son, it was very slow progress.

Dianne Craft

Dianne Craft is an educational therapist with over 35 years of experience who has designed a program to teach the right-brained learner according to his or her unique learning style. She is recommended by HSLDA. We used her program many years ago and were happy with the results but again, with a profoundly dyslexic son, needed something more intense, direct and systematic than what Dianne Craft had to offer. I still refer to her articles and her web site for tips on teaching the right-brained children. Dianne Craft is a wealth of information.

We've learned what dyslexia is and perhaps more importantly what methods really work to teach a dyslexic person to read. Next up, we will take a look at how the special education process in the public schools works and how to help your child get the help he or she needs.

Chapter 5: Navigating the Public School System

If your child is struggling with reading in the public school, you will want to attempt to work with your child's school personnel to get your child the help they need to get up to speed in reading, writing and spelling as soon as possible. Many parents delay seeking help for their children because they don't trust their intuition that something may be wrong. They fear their lack of knowledge and defer to teachers whom they respect as educational experts.

This delay is understandable, but it must not be done. It is critical to get your child the help they need quickly. There are teaching methods that work and the sooner your child starts, the less trouble he or she will have catching up and the more likely he or she will be to avoid some of the pitfalls of falling behind.

No one knows your child as well as you do, therefore you will be their best advocate to help them get the kind of teaching/tutoring they will need to be successful throughout their school years.

There are two things to keep in mind during this process. First, all dyslexics can learn to read (even though it may not seem like it at times!) with the right methods and lots of practice. Second, early intervention is best. Don't wait to get them the help they need.

The Basics

All public schools are required by federal law to have a plan in place to "identify, locate and evaluate" children who may have a disability and need special education. In addition, each state across the country has their own eligibility criteria. These laws were put in place to help protect both you and your child and do the best that can be done to help your child succeed.

A large part of a successful learning experience for your child will hinge on how well you understand your family's rights and how well you are able to communicate and relate with your child's public school personnel.

In the previous chapters, you learned that dyslexia is somewhat complex and manifests differently in different people. Teachers and schools are dealing with large numbers of children with a wide variety of individual needs both physical and academic. Though their heart may be to help kids and the system is set up to support them, managing each individual with specific needs is going to be necessarily difficult as evidenced by the enormous body of laws surrounding the entire special education process. Approach your child's school with a large dose of understanding mixed with a good amount of assertiveness, when necessary, and you will have more success.

How the Special Education Process Works

The Key Terms

Being a successful advocate for your child will require that you become familiar with the laws and terminology used to describe the special education process. Here is a list of common terms that you may encounter along the way. Some of these terms have not been introduced yet. This glossary is placed here, early in the chapter, for you to refer back to as and when needed.

504 Plan: A civil rights law that prohibits discrimination on the basis of a person's disability by programs and activities that receive federal funds. A 504 plan outlines a plan of instructional services available for students with learning disabilities in the general education classroom.

Accommodations: Changes that allow a person with a disability to participate fully in an activity. Examples include, extended time, different test format, and alterations to a classroom.

Assessment or Evaluation: Term used to describe the testing and diagnostic processes leading up to the development of an appropriate treatment plan (see IEP) for a student with special education needs.

Disability: Physical or mental impairment that substantially limits one or more major life activities.

Due Process: Special education term used to describe the process where parents may disagree with the program recommendations of the school district. The notice must be given in writing within 30 days. IDEA provides two methods for resolving disputes, mediation or fair hearing.

Free and Appropriate Public Education (FAPE): Special education and related services are provided at public expense, without charge to the parents.

Impartial due process hearing is a meeting between parents and the school district. Each side presents its position, and a hearing officer decides what the appropriate educational program is, based on requirements in law.

Individuals with Disabilities Education Act (IDEA 2004): The original legislation was written in 1975 guaranteeing students with disabilities a free and appropriate public education and the right to be educated with their non-disabled peers. Congress has reauthorized this federal law. The most recent revision occurred in 2004.

Individualized Education Plan (IEP): Special education term outlined by IDEA to define the written document that states the disabled child's goals, objectives and services for students receiving special education.

Independent Educational Evaluation (IEE): A school district is required by law to conduct assessments for students who may be eligible for special education. If the parent disagrees with the results of a school district's evaluation conducted on their child, they have the right to request an independent educational evaluation (IEE). The district must provide parents with information about how to obtain an IEE. An independent educational evaluation means an evaluation conducted by a qualified examiner who is not employed by the school district. Public expense means the school district pays for the full cost of the evaluation and that it is provided at no cost to the parent.

Least Restrictive Environment (LRE): The placement of a special needs student in a manner promoting the maximum possible interaction with the general school population. Placement options are offered on a continuum including regular classroom with no support services, regular classroom with support services, designated instruction services, special day classes and private special education programs.

Mediation: A meeting between parents and the school district with an impartial person, called a mediator, who helps both sides come to an agreement that each finds acceptable.

OSEP: Office of Special Education Programs (part of the US Education Department)

Response to Intervention (RTI): Set up under the regulations in IDEA to move schools away from the old discrepancy requirement for identification of learning disabilities (SLD). The discrepancy requirement meant that there had to be a 'severe discrepancy' between a child's academic achievement and intellectual ability. This is a good indicator of a SLD but kids had to fail for a long period of time to be eligible. RTI requires that schools assess a child's eligibility for testing and services based on his or her response to scientific, research-based interventions (classroom instruction) rather than on the discrepancy model alone. This avoids waiting until the child is behind.

Special Education Services: Additional services, support, programs, specialized placements or environments to ensure that all students' educational needs are provided for.

Specific Learning Disability (SLD): Special education term used to define a disorder in one or more of the basic psychological processes involved in understanding or using language spoken or written that may manifest itself in an imperfect ability to listen, think, speak, read, write, spell or do mathematical equations.

National Parent Technical Assistance Center Network (PTAC)
www.parentcenternetwork.org/national/ resources.html: Organization funded by the US

Department of Education to provide training and information to parents of children with disabilities. Has links to support groups and information on the special education laws in every state.

The Laws

Since 1975 every child with a disability has been entitled to a free and appropriate pubic education (FAPE) designed to meet his or her individual educational needs under the rules and regulations of the Individuals with Disabilities Education Act (IDEA). This federal law governs all special education services and serves to guarantee an appropriate specialized education plan for all students aged 3-21 who meet the criteria for eligibility.

According to the Learning Disabilities Association of America (LDA), approximately 3 million children, nearly 6%, receive special education and related services because of learning disabilities.

Some kids with special needs do not receive services under IDEA but are served under Section 504 of the Rehabilitation Act of 1973. Section 504, a civil rights law, prohibits discrimination on the basis of a person's disability by programs and activities that receive federal funds. A 504 plan outlines a plan of instructional services available for students with learning disabilities in the general education classroom. Students with ADHD often have a 504 plan in place to offer them accommodations to allow them to complete their assignments like the other kids in the classroom. Accommodations are changes in the way the child completes their regular school work that allows for an 'even playing field' so-to-speak. Examples of classroom accommodations for dyslexia include allowing for larger print, books on tape, allowing verbal responses, untimed tests, providing notetakers, or testing at a specific time of day. In this way, students with learning disabilities are given the same coursework and graded with the same standard as other students. Schools must provide these children with reasonable accommodations. For some children, appropriate accommodations are enough to allow them to be successful in the general classroom environment.

Before Requesting an Evaluation

You can request an evaluation at any time. In the interests of building a solid relationship with your child's school personnel, it may be beneficial to talk to the teacher first. Discuss your child's unique situation and get feedback on the circumstances and variables, including your child's performance, within the classroom. You also may want to talk to your school principal. Find out what special education services your child's school has available and which instructional approaches they use. Request a written copy of your district's special education procedures. Working with your child's school personnel in an understanding way will help to foster a truly collaborative team best suited to help your child in the long run. Get informed. Contact the National Parent Technical Assistance Center Network (PTAC). They can help you understand how the special education process works in your state.

How to Request an Evaluation

Before your child can receive any special services through their school, they will need to be evaluated or tested. This type of evaluation is typically administered by a public school psychologist and must include a variety of assessment tools such as an IQ test, behavior, mental health, communication and motor abilities assessments as well as tests of academic achievement.

When parents, school staff or a student thinks they may have some kind of learning issue, they can make a request for an evaluation. This request must be made in writing and give the school permission to conduct the evaluation. The letter should briefly state the reasons that you suspect a learning disability and request a full evaluation. Date, sign and keep a copy for your records before sending it to the school principal.

Once the school has received your request for an evaluation, the school district must do one of two things. They may agree to the assessment in which case they have 60 days (in most states) from the date you give your written consent to perform the evaluation. Or, the school may deny your request for an evaluation if they feel that your child's struggles are not due to a learning disability. They must provide written explanation for their determination.

If the school refuses to evaluate your child, be sure to ask them, in writing, why they do not suspect that your child may have a learning disability. This is called Prior Written Notice. Once you receive this you have the right to file a due process complaint with your state's Department of Education. Forms and detailed information should be available at your state's Department of Education web site.

Parents at this point may opt to have their child tested privately. If you choose to have your child privately evaluated, the school is not responsible for the cost unless, in some states, a diagnosis is made.

The exact tests and assessments that your child receives vary from state to state and even within districts. It depends on who is giving the evaluation.

A Note on Record Keeping

It is extremely important that you as the parent keep complete records of all communication during the special education process. This should include a communication log of all conversations that take place regarding your child. Other types of records that parents should maintain:

- Report cards and progress reports
- Standardized test scores
- Evaluation results
- Medical records related to disability or ability to learn
- Any IEPs or other services such as 504 plans
- Awards received by the child
- Notices of disciplinary actions
- Notes on your child's behavior or progress
- Letters or notes to and from the school or teacher, special educators, evaluators, and administrators
- Notices of meetings scheduled
- Student handbook and policies
- Attendance records
- Calendar of meetings
- Samples of schoolwork
- A detailed communication log:

- records of meetings and their outcomes
- dates you sent or received important documents
- dates you gave the school important information
- dates of suspension or other disciplinary actions
- notes on telephone conversations including dates, name of person you spoke with and a short description of the conversation

Once your child is evaluated:

A team of education professionals will review the results of the evaluation with you. The results of the evaluation will determine if your child is eligible for special education services but not necessarily give a specific diagnosis. Special education services are additional services, support, programs, specialized placements or environments to ensure that al students' educational needs are provided for. These are provided at no cost to the parents.

If your child is not determined to be eligible, you will be notified and the process stops. You do have the right to disagree with the results of the evaluation and eligibility decision. In this case you have the right to an Independent Educational Evaluation (IEE).

Someone who does not work for the school district completes the IEE and the school district must pay for it or show at a due process hearing, that their prior determination of no eligibility was accurate. As always, make any request for an IEE in writing and keep a copy for your records.

If your child is determined to be eligible for special education services, you and school staff will plan your child's Individualized Education Program (IEP) at an IEP team meeting. Some states may have a different name for the IEP team meeting.

An IEP lists any special services your child needs including goals your child is expected to achieve within the year. It will also include benchmarks to be met along the way. The team will decide what services are needed and how and where they will be received. There may be more than one meeting and you can request a meeting any time you wish. Before attending this meeting, you will want to be as well informed as possible about your child's specific disability. *That is the purpose of this book!*

Special education law allows for your child to be taught in the Least Restrictive Environment (LRE) appropriate for your chid. This is to ensure that the special needs child is having the most 'normal' school experience possible while at the same time receiving the most effective instruction in the most productive environment. Generally this mean keeping the child in the general classroom as much as possible. This is the school's preferred arrangement unless the IEP team decides that, even with special aids and services, the child is not experiencing success within the classroom. Other placements include receiving some support services outside the classroom or special day programs and even private special education programs.

If at any point, you as the parent, disagree with placement and services provided for your child, you have the right to use your due process rights.

If you agree with the IEP, your child will receive the services that are written in the IEP. You will be updated on your child's progress as often as every other child in class. You can always request a meeting if you feel there is any problem or changes needed.

The IEP team meets at least once a year to discuss progress and make any changes to your child's goals or services. If you ever disagree with any changes, you should do so in writing. Your child will continue to receive services as listed in the previous IEP until you and the IEP team reach an agreement. If you continue to disagree, you have several options including asking for additional testing or an IEE or using your due process rights.

Special education services will continue as long as the team agrees that they are needed. A re-evaluation is done at least once every three years to redetermine eligibility if you and school personnel deem more services necessary.

Understanding Your Rights

Special education law is set up to protect and provide for your special needs child in the best possible way. Not all school personnel are well-versed in these laws. It is important that you know and understand your rights during this process.

Your child has the right to a free and appropriate public education (FAPE). If you suspect that your child may have a learning disability, you have the right to request that your child be evaluated to determine if he or she is eligible for special education services. This must be done at no cost to you. This testing is available to any child in the district, whether they are schooled in the home or in a private school.

Teachers may recommend an evaluation as well but the school must have your written consent before any part of the evaluation is started.

If the school refuses to give your child an evaluation, they must do so in writing giving an explanation for the decision. They must give you information about how to appeal their decision in the letter.

All tests and interviews must be conducted in your child's native language.

Parents have the right to be part of the evaluation team that decides which information is needed to determine whether or not your child is eligible for services.

You have a right to all reports and paperwork associated with your child.

You have the right to obtain your own evaluation called an Independent Education Evaluation from a qualified professional to challenge the findings of the school evaluation team. If a learning disability is diagnosed, you may be able to be reimbursed.

You have the right to have your child's evaluation be completed within a specific period of time, specifically within 60 days of your written consent.

Once your child is determined to be eligible for special education and related services, you and your child have the right to attend and participate in a meeting to design and Individualized Education Program (IEP) within 30 days of being found eligible.

An IEP should set reasonable goals for your child and clearly state the services that the school will provide. People involved in the IEP process are you, your child, your child's teachers, and a representative from the school who is qualified to recommend and supervise special programs.

During an IEP meeting, the IEP team will set up goals for any related services such as occupational therapy that may be necessary. The team should specify how often and for how long these services will be provided.

Subsequent IEP meetings must be held once a year and a comprehensive re-evaluation must be done every three years. You may request an IEP meeting at any time.

You can request an advisor be present to help you understand both your rights and your responsibilities during the entire special education process.

Your child has a right to receive services within the general classroom with children without learning disabilities when at all possible. This is called the least restrictive environment.

Your child's IEP should include recommendations for any assistive technology services or devices that may be of benefit to your child. The school should provide the device and train your child to use it. School districts must give parents a written copy of their special education procedures. It should outline the steps for any due process hearing or mediation.

Understanding Limitations of the Special Education Process

Despite the elaborate legal underpinnings of special education law, many parents say that their children are not getting effective literacy remediation in schools. This plays out in several different ways:

1. The school doesn't acknowledge that the child needs extra help or remediation, often saying that the student is 'coping'.

2. The school acknowledges a concern about the student's progress but has no specialist support to offer.
3. The school acknowledges concern and promises to offer support but, in practice, this ends up being ineffective for the following reasons:
   - Not frequent enough or long enough
   - Provided by untrained people
   - Not the treatment that the child needs

Why Do Schools Struggle to Provide the Proper Support?

Special needs kids are taught in the mainstream classroom commonly believed to be the best or Least Restrictive Environment. However, teachers in the regular classroom say that they do not receive enough specialist training for special education needs in general or for Specific Learning Disabilities like dyslexia and feel ill-equipped to help these kids.

Teachers do not know enough about dyslexia and are unable to:
- Identify the warning signs in children who may have dyslexia

- Assess or screen for dyslexia
- Understand effective intervention methods
- Provide appropriate remediation

Parents assume that their child's teachers have this expertise and assume that appropriate help will be given through the school.

There are other factors that hinder schools providing the proper interventions for kids with dyslexia. The evaluation process can be confusing. Children can wait many months before testing. Special education funds are limited and schools are forced to prioritize. Dyslexia may not seem severe enough to reach the top of the list. Teachers trained in special education methods are expensive, if you can find one.

Understanding the use of the term dyslexia

Many parents with children in the public schools are frustrated that the school will diagnose their child with a 'Specific Learning Disability' (SLD) but that they seem unwilling to even recognize the term dyslexia. They are concerned that without that specific diagnosis, their child will not receive the appropriate help for their reading struggles. While Federal law does recognize the term dyslexia, most schools are only working with their own state laws which may or may not recognize the term. To learn more about your states education laws visit the National Parent Technical Assistance Center Network or PTAC. http://www.parentcenterhub.org/ptacs/

In 20 U.S.C. section 1401(30)(B) of IDEA 2004, federal law defines the disorders included in the Specific Learning Disability (SLD) category as "perceptual disabilities, brain injury, minimal brain dysfunction, **dyslexia** and developmental aphasia".

The use of the terms dyslexia or specific learning disability are understood differently depending on who you are and what your purpose is:

- *Education law* is broad in its scope as it needs to cover a wide range of learning issues both physical and developmental and therefore uses both the term specific learning disability and dyslexia.
- *Researchers*, like Sally Shaywitz and her team at Yale University, conduct research and write books such as *Overcoming Dyslexia* and call this condition dyslexia.

- *Doctors and psychologists* are using the DSM-IV to derive a diagnosis code. The DSM-IV is published by the American Psychiatric Association to provide clinicians with a set of criteria for diagnosing various disorders. The DSM-IV says, "...individuals with Reading Disorder (which has also been called 'dyslexia') have reading achievement measured by individually administered standardized tests that is substantially below what would be expected given the individual's age, measured intelligence, and schooling.
- *Teachers* may refer to the language in their own states education law which may or may not refer to the exact diagnosis of dyslexia.
- *Parents* are reading books and web sites that refer to their child's reading struggles as dyslexia.

This confusion over the term dyslexia is an excellent example of the need for enhanced education for everyone involved in the education process, especially those who are in the classrooms working one on one with our kids. If teachers and administrators had more in-depth instruction in the different types of learning disabilities, special education laws, as well as their diagnosis and treatment there would be far fewer communication gaps.

Remember, the school's fundamental goal remains the same: to determine eligibility for special education services, *not diagnose dyslexia.* If your child has been determined to have a learning disability you have the same legal rights to an IEP and other classroom accommodations as you would with a more specific diagnosis of dyslexia. Also the solution is the same. Your child needs a specialized education geared to his or her learning style. In most cases, those techniques are the same as are commonly used for dyslexic children.

Cutting through the confusion

How can you cut through the confusion and get help for your child? Here are some suggestions:

- When seeking help for your child, be sure to consider the source when you hear (or don't hear) the term "dyslexia" used.

- When communicating with your child's teachers, find out what terms they use to describe dyslexia so you can start speaking the same language. Ask specific questions, and expect specific answers.

- Remember that the legal, medical, and scientific references to dyslexia aren't always consistent with each other. When you need to understand the details of a legal statute or research study to learn more about your child's learning difficulty, try digging deeper to learn more about the specific language processing problem being discussed.

Parents should collaborate with their child's school as much as possible before seeking outside help to see if they will be able to help meet the child's needs. There are three important factors to focus on in this process:

- Diagnosis: What is the underlying problem (regardless of whether it is called dyslexia or SLD)

- Methods: Which methods your school intends to use. Are they research-based? Orton-Gillingham?
- Progress: Is enough progress being made.

It's likely that the media portrayal and public perception of dyslexia will remain confusing for years to come. Don't waste time and energy reacting to what you see as misinformation in the press! Instead, invest your energy in getting the straight story from the people and resources that can **directly** help your child.

When your child's needs are not being met

Many schools offer what they believe is the best available approach for teaching your special needs child that fits within their budget constraints. Teachers want to use the best available methods but they may be misinformed as to what those are or inadequately trained to implement them.

Schools also have many children to care for. You are ultimately the only one who knows your child's unique history including childhood experiences and level of previous instruction.

You cannot afford to be swayed by advice or opinions that are misinformed or your child will lose valuable time. You must challenge (with respect) what you believe is not working well.

Your goal is to have the school offer a program, monitor how effective it is and then advocate if the program is not working. Often, students will make some progress so schools will feel that enough is being done. It is a common mistake to allow your child to continue in a program that is not working quick enough.

Understand that schools and their administrators have a difficult job to do. They have to balance all the needs of all the students in the school while dealing with underfunded budgets. No matter how you finally choose to find help for your dyslexic child, it will be hard. Whether you work within the confines of your child's school, tutor them at home, find an outside tutor or homeschool them, there is no magic cure for overcoming dyslexia. It will require dedication, perseverance and a lot of hard work.

Exhaust school resources first, but be prepared to take action when time is passing without resolution of your concerns. There are other options. The next two chapters talk about two other options besides relying solely on your child's school. Chapter 6 will take a look the benefits to homeschooling your child with dyslexia including everything you need to know to get started. Chapter 7 talks about when and how to hire a private educational therapist or tutor to help your child.

Resources

Although it may feel like it at times, you are not alone in your quest to find the best possible help for your struggling reader. The following organizations are a wealth of information to help you along the way.

Building the Legacy: IDEA 2004 (idea.ed.gov/)
The U.S. Department of Education, Office of Special Education Programs website provides access to the IDEA 2004 statute,regulations, and helpful information.

National Association of School Psychologists
(www.nasponline.org/)
NASP's has a variety of resource materials and
helpful fact sheets for parents. See collection of
papers addressing the role of parents and school
teams in RTI models: New Roles in Response to
Intervention: Creating Success for Schools and
Children (
www.nasponline.org/advocacy/rtifactsheets.aspx)

National Center for Learning for Learning Disabilities
(www.ld.org/)
NCLD offers parents helpful information and
resources on school-related topics and advocacy
information.

National Joint Committee on Learning Disabilities:
(NJCLD www.ldonline.org/njcld) The NJCLD is
comprised of 13 organizations committed to the
education and welfare of individuals with learning
disabilities.

From Emotions to Advocacy: The Special Education
Survival Guide (www.fetaweb.org) A treasure of
resources for learning effective advocacy skills within
the public school. Excellent!

National Association of Protections and Advocacy
Systems www.napas.org

Chapter 6: Homeschooling Your Dyslexic Child

According to the International Dyslexia Association, *"dyslexic students need direct, systematic and individual instruction in reading and spelling and traditional schools do not always provide adequate levels of service"*. We saw in the last chapter that although Educational Law is set up to protect the rights of a child to a free and appropriate education, it often fails to do so. Are there other options?

Our family's experiences teaching children with dyslexia is somewhat unusual in that we have homeschooled for the past 20 years. Of our 8 children, 7 of them have some degree of dyslexia whether mild, moderate, or profound. A common fear that parents have of homeschooling their dyslexic child is that they believe that they are ill-prepared or unqualified to adequately teach them. I struggled with this fear for many years. When our oldest two kids were 9 and 7 years old, our family took a three year sailing trip. Our 9 year old was still not reading well and the 7 year old was following in his footsteps. We had explored several treatment options but they were expensive and had little evidence that they were truly effective.

While we were on our sailing trip, we rented our house out to a family with children our own kids' ages. They were enrolled in the local public school that our kids would have attended had we chosen to go that route. We found out later that their 8 year old daughter had all of the classic signs of dyslexia. She struggled to read but her teacher was unaware of dyslexia symptoms and misjudged her as a lazy girl who just didn't try hard enough. She tried to motivate her by forcing her to read in out loud and mocking her in front of the entire class. She was teased and laughed at to the point of feigning illness so that she would not have to go to school. Certainly this is not the case in every situation, however, it is far too common. The teacher simply did not know how to teach kids like this family's daughter who was a bright girl who learned differently or that these differences were signs that she needed outside help.

The bottom line in all of this is that regular, credentialed schoolroom teachers have had little to no training on learning disabilities; what the warning signs are or how they are best treated. We saw in the last chapter that while the law is set up to help kids with learning disabilities, it is not an easy, straight-forward process. Frankly, no matter how or where you choose to have your child educated, teaching the dyslexic child is difficult, requiring a lot of creativity, perseverance as well as effective methods.

Over the past 20 years that we have homeschooled our kids with dyslexia, I have learned by experience that not only is it possible, in my humble opinion, it is the best option if it is within your power to do so.

Benefits to Homeschooling a Child With Dyslexia
Besides allowing your child the freedom to learn at their own pace and using the methods best suited to their learning styles, there are other reasons why homeschooling is a better environment for educating your child who learns differently.

- Allows for the necessary individualized instruction in all subject areas: reading, spelling, composition and comprehension.
- Allows for kids to focus on areas of interest and for lessons to be planned around those interests.
- Allows for freedom from being measured against peers, day in and day out, with no learning difficulties.
- Allows for your child to work at their own pace using resources (See Appendix A) that work best with their individual strengths.
- Homeschooling necessarily avoids the rigid scheduling and standardized testing {and the practice of teaching to the test} that is required in the public schools.

There is no one who knows, or cares for, your child like you do. The resources are out there. It can be done. How do you get started?

How to Get Started Homeschooling

According to the National Home Education Research Institute (NRERI) there were over 2 million children being homeschooled, that is, parent-led, home-based education, in the United States in the year 2010. Home educated kids score above average on achievement tests regardless of their parents' level of formal education or their family's household income. The NHERI also found that homeschool students are increasingly being actively recruited by colleges. For more of the NHERI's research facts on homeschooling, please visit their web site at www.nheri.org/researchfacts.pdf

General Homeschool How To's and Legalities

Homeschooling is increasingly mainstream and, yes, completely legal. To get started homeschooling you will want to find out the laws in your individual state. Home School Legal Defense (HSLDA.org) is a good place to start.

When planning your instruction, research resources suited toward your child's learning style. There is a comprehensive list of homeschooling resources for teaching dyslexics at the end of the book.

Consider getting outside help, beginning with testing, from an educational psychologist and possibly tutoring from a trained educational therapist who will work alongside you as you homeschool. See the next chapter on exactly how to do this.

Get plugged in to a good homeschool support group (resources available on the Homeschool Legal Defense web site www.homeschoollegaldefense.org). Find other families who are teaching kids who learn differently who can support you and guide you along the way.

Homeschool Methods

The traditional text book, workbook, quiz and test format is the easiest way to organize and manage the teacher-to-student ratio in the public or private schoolroom – mainly for organizational purposes. Everybody has the same assignments. Everyone is required to complete the same work. There is little room for individualized instruction, even if there was understanding of the benefits to doing so. There are many different homeschool methods.

Traditional: Closest to what you find in a traditional classroom. May be good if you have recently brought your kids out of the public school system. Heavily teacher driven.

Unit Studies: Integrates all subjects into one theme. Good for combining subjects with multiple ages, is hands-on and activity based. Good for teaching multiple ages at once.

Charlotte Mason: A whole child approach that is based around reading 'living books" but includes focus on short, intense class meetings, nature study, narration, copy work, and the study of fine arts. The goal of the Charlotte Mason method is to instill a love of learning and a curiosity about life in the student. This method has many characteristics that appeal to the dyslexic learner.

Classical: Based on the three stages of intellectual development (grammar, logic, rhetoric) and relies heavily on the Classics in literature for the base of study. The goal of the Classical Method is to create critical thinkers.

Eclectic: A mix of many methods – usually gained by experience of what works best in your home. Nice for accommodating multiple learning styles.

Unschooling: Child directed, no text books yet purposeful.

Finding the Best Homeschool Curriculum for Your Family

With so many excellent curriculums to choose from, how can you find the best materials for your family? Taking into account learning styles and homeschool methods that appeal to you and your students, you can begin to search for curriculums that are the best fit.

General Tips

- Search online for curriculums that fit your family's learning styles
- Read reviews – see Cathy Duffy's web site at cathyduffyreviews.com
- Talk to other homeschool moms of dyslexic kids (or read their blogs!)
- Look for curriculums with audio options

• Look for curriculums with hands-on activities

Don't Hesitate to Use Technology

With so much technology out there for enhancing education, don't think that using these methods is somehow inferior to classic pen and paper learning. From multi-sensory iPad apps, to text-to-speech programs to speech-to-text and on, these are tools that can greatly enhance your child's learning while they continue to perfect their reading and writing by more traditional means. The Resource section at the end of this book contains a list of my favorite resources for teaching my dyslexic family, including some of the latest and greatest technology that we use.

Finding Balance:

There will be a homeschool method that appeals to you, the teacher, and another one that will appeal to your child, the student. Usually, the style(s) that you find the most interesting will be the most effective. I am a classic left-brained, just-tell-me-how-many-pages-to-fill-in kind of girl. I like the order and clarity of workbooks. My kids, however, struggle with that type of learning. My right-brained, creative children would rather act out a scene from a certain period of history than write a paper on it. This is completely overwhelming to me. We have had to find compromise in our curriculum so that they are learning and I am not stressing out!

General Learning Preferences for Dyslexic Learners

Dyslexic kids, in general, do better with:

- shorter, intense teaching sessions
- auditory learning {audio books, discussion, educational DVDs}
- oral work or discussion of material

Dyslexic learners {in general} don't do so well with:

- lots of writing {look for narration exercises, arts-based assignments}
- learning by reading {look for curriculums with video or audio lectures}
- spelling lists
- rote memorization

While all people (dyslexic or not) have certain ways that they learn best, using a multi-sensory approach (combining seeing, saying, listening and doing) will help your child learn faster and enhance his or her ability to retain new information. Also, making accommodations for learning styles should not exclude learning by other methods. If your child learns better through the auditory channel, great. Use auditory methods when you can but still be working on improving reading speed and comprehension on a daily basis.

Don't be Afraid to 'Tweek' Things

Most homeschool curriculums can be adapted to fit alternate learning styles. This year, I have two 9th-graders who are working through a rigorous Integrated Physics and Chemistry curriculum. I wanted something taught on video. This appeals to their auditory learning preference. However, their accompanying reading assignments are difficult and full of vocabulary that they have never heard before. We began the year plugging their (online) reading assignments into a text-to-speech app on our iPad. This was helpful, because they could follow along as the iPad read their assignment. However, the content was still confusing to them so, rather than immediately list the curriculum on eBay (which I have done plenty of times!) I decided to sit one or two days per week and read the assignment with them. We stopped whenever there was something we didn't understand, looked up vocabulary words or better yet, watched a video or two on the <u>Kahn Academy web site</u>. {Oh my, this site is a homeschool mom's dream come true!} We also had a lot of discussions about what we were learning and finding connections to things that we already knew. By creatively working with our curriculum, we were able to make it work for us. Will I buy this curriculum for Biology next year? Maybe not, but we are learning how to learn which is a large part of homeschooling, especially for the dyslexic.

The Power of Interest-Driven Learning
I can not stress this enough. All children need to learn the basic flow of history, how to write a coherent paper and how to think critically. Step back and look

at the big picture. If you can combine a particular interest of your child say from your history studies (battles, clothing, art, etc) and combine it with their writing assignment for English, you have captured their interest. In my experience, my kids were much more willing to push through their learning difficulties when they were motivated by what they were learning!

Truths About Finding the Right Homeschool Curriculum

There is no magic cure for dyslexia. A dyslexic child will become a dyslexic adult. However, all children {and adults} can learn to read and write. Dr. Maryanne Wolf, Director of the Center for Reading and Language Research at Tufts University has said "There are no universally effective (reading) programs, but there are knowledgable principles that need to be incorporated in all programs about how we teach written language." Teaching to your child's strengths with research-based methods customized to your child's learning style and centered around his or her interests along with helping your child learn compensation techniques will go a long way to providing the level of literacy needed to become a successful adult.

There will be days of frustration when you feel that nothing is 'working' and want to give up. Rome was not conquered in a day! Press on and you will see, not only the advantages to homeschooling your dyslexic child, but the success.

It may take several tries to get a good fit that works well with your family. Don't be too hasty or too slow to replace a curriculum. Just because it works for everyone else or got great reviews, doesn't mean it will be a good fit for your family.

Chapter 7: Hiring a Private Tutor or Educational Therapist

Teaching reading to a dyslexic learner takes time, dedication and hard work. There is no quick fix and if anyone tells you that there is they are probably trying to sell you something that you don't need.   Many parents find it difficult to get their child the help that they need from the public school. Maybe you are homeschooling but you don't have the time or the confidence to teach your child as well as you would like. It was once believed that a child may outgrow his or her reading struggles. Research has now shown that this is not the case. Dyslexic kids grow up to be dyslexic adults. By intervening early on, the gaps in learning can be mostly avoided along with the emotional difficulties that inevitably follow being markedly 'different' from peers. If you are unable to provide the intense, early intervention that your dyslexic child needs, you may want to consider hiring a tutor.

Dyslexia: Mild, Moderate or Profound

Dyslexia varies in severity. Two of my children are what can be called profoundly dyslexic. They are both very bright and creative but struggled way more than my other dyslexic kids learning reading, writing and spelling. Two of my kids were moderately dyslexic. They struggled with reading but after time and with perseverance, were able to read and spell well by working with me at home. One of my kids was mildly dyslexic and though she was behind her peers for a time, is currently working at and above her grade level.

Individual strengths and weaknesses vary within each child. Learning styles and personality can have a major effect on how well a child responds to instruction. There came a time in one of our children's life that we knew he was simply not progressing at an acceptable pace and that we needed help. He was already in 5th grade but still unable to read much of anything on his own. The first step to getting help is getting some kind of assessment of your child's individual learning profile.

What are their specific strengths? What are their areas of weakness? Having your child tested will give the educational therapist the picture of your child that he or she needs to effectively tutor them.

How to Know if an Educational Therapist or Tutor is Qualified

If you are considering hiring a professional tutor for your child you will want to know what their qualifications are. An educational therapist should have the right educational background, special training and experience working with dyslexic children. Many of the same principles apply as for choosing an educational tester. Arrange to meet with the potential tutor and ask them about their training, experience and involvement in ongoing training courses that will keep them abreast of the latest research. In general, any educational therapist you hire should use all of the research-based methods that were discussed in Chapter 4: Reading Instruction That Works.

How to Know if a Particular Tutor is the Right Person to Work With Your Child

Hiring a professional tutor for your child is expensive and, more importantly, your child will be putting a lot of faith in the tutor you select. Knowing that the tutor you choose is qualified is important but if your child does not trust, respect or like their tutor (or vice versa) your time and money will be wasted. You must feel that the potential tutor will be able to build a good rapport with you and your child. Educational therapy is necessarily difficult and there will be days that your child will be upset, even angry, at the struggles that they are facing. Having a tutor that your child feels is working alongside him or her, and believing in them, will help them to be able to persevere through the difficult times. Meet and interview any potential tutor to see if their personal style and expertise is a good match for your child.

FAQs

What About Testing

The purpose of testing and evaluation is to find out why your child is having difficulties learning and what specific path should be taken to best help. Bring your child's test results to your prospective tutor to discuss their thoughts on and strategies for helping your child.

How Long Will it Take?

How long your child needs educational therapy depends on how severe your child's dyslexia is and how often they meet with their tutor. A minimum of two sessions, if not three, per week is recommended. Tutoring should, ideally, continue until your child is working independently at his or her grade level. This could take two to three years or even more, especially if you start when your child is older. Our profoundly dyslexic son spent two years in one tutoring program, before being tested. Yes, we learned by experience the importance of testing before tutoring! Although the program and tutor were excellent, progress was extremely slow. We had him tested and learned that because of his low auditory and visual processing speeds, he needed a different method that spent time strengthening these areas. He just began his 3rd year at a place whose methods are better suited for his particular weaknesses and he has made remarkable progress.

Costs

Costs for a professional educational therapist vary from state to state and city to city. Many people who choose this area as a profession, have a heart for these kids and see their role as a ministry of sorts. Both tutors we have used have had family members that struggled with dyslexia, thus their passion for helping others. Our family's philosophy has been, "Why save for college if they aren't even going to go there because of their unresolved learning issues?" In our experience, the time and money spent on educational therapy was worth every penny for our kids who have needed it.

Benefits

How well your child overcomes his or her dyslexia has the potential to have a huge impact on their future success and happiness. Knowing (and believing) that they are not stupid, that they can learn and that with perseverance and the right support, they can have success, will benefit them greatly in life. Successful dyslexics are known for their perseverance. I know, I am married to one! The investment in their learning while they are young is really an investment in their future as well – a future of learning.

Resources

To find a reputable educational therapist in your area, ask your local school, homeschool group or, better yet, another family with a dyslexic child who is experiencing success with a local tutor. You can also contact one of the following national organizations for a referral:

International Dyslexia Association   www.interdys.org

Academic Language Therapy Association_
www.altaread.org

Association of Educational Therapists
www.aetonline.org

A Note About NILD

Two of our kids are now receiving educational therapy from our local National Institute for Learning Development (NILD.org). Our oldest was not progressing well and we saw signs in our younger daughter of the same severity of symptoms. We enrolled our daughter in the early intervention program and our son in the NILD program. Our son advanced 5-6 grade levels in one year. Our daughter (now 9) is reading well and has a high level of confidence though she still needs to work at her spelling. I highly recommend their program because they really do look at the whole child. They spend a lot of time developing and strengthening the auditory and visual memory through games and other means. They teach the kids HOW to think which has been of huge benefit for my two highly dyslexic kids. Please visit the NILD web site for more information or to find a tutor near you.

Lindamood Bell LIPS Program

The Lindamood Phoneme Sequencing (LiPS) program is designed to teach students the skills they need to decode words and to identify individual sounds and blends in words. Activities begin with helping students to discover the lip, tongue, and mouth actions needed to produce specific sounds. After students are able to produce, label, and organize the sounds with their mouths, subsequent activities in sequencing, reading, and spelling use the oral aspects of sounds to identify and order them within words. The program also offers direct instruction in letter patterns, sight words, and context clues in reading. LiPS® is designed for emergent readers in kindergarten through grade 3 or for struggling, dyslexic readers.

Chapter 8: Preparing Your Student With Dyslexia for College Success

If college is on the horizon for your dyslexic student, you may be concerned about whether or not they are prepared to handle the rigors of a traditional college course of study. In my experience, all students with dyslexia can succeed in college. These next few chapters will elaborate on the skills needed for a student with dyslexia to succeed in college so that you can begin to prepare now.

There are programs, accommodations, laws and even scholarships for the dyslexic student. Although college will be much like high school for the dyslexic student, requiring more work and effort than students without dyslexia, many dyslexics have successfully graduated from college.

Despite difficulties processing the written word, with the right planning and preparation, your dyslexic child can achieve his or her dream of earning a college degree.

As I researched further into each of these topics, I began to be so excited! There are so many options for our kids who learn differently. I hope these chapters will be as encouraging for you to read as it was for me to write.

Some things for you to be thinking about as you begin to consider college for your student:

- Why do you want your child to go to college?
- What is the goal?
- Is your child motivated to go to college?
- Is there another path that may serve your dyslexic student better than college such as a trade school or starting their own business?

These questions are not posed to cause doubt, but rather to make sure that you are not just doing what everybody else is doing, but truly seeking the best path for your child. Talk these things over with your kids. Find out where they stand on furthering their education. There are many options and many helps for your kids. Anything is possible!

The types of skills needed to be successful in college can seem overwhelming, especially if you have dyslexia. If college is something that your child is serious about pursuing, developing these skills can be a part of your high school curriculum. Whether your student is homeschooled or attends a private or public school, many of these skills can be taught and practiced right from home!

As with many other subjects, dyslexics learn better with explicit instruction and lots of practice. This will help your student find the most efficient strategies for learning; the methods that are best-suited to his or her learning style.

Academic Skills

Reading

College students can be expected to read as much as 200 pages per week. For many dyslexics, including my own dyslexic kids, this can seem like a death sentence to college success. Remember, reading 200 pages is in addition to class time, social time, study time and some semblance of sleep time.

There are many tools available to help students get that reading done and understand it as well. See Appendix # on Preparing Your Dyslexic Student for College Level Reading for more tips on practicing college level reading skills.

Students should be able to comprehend and summarize college-level reading material. Despite myths that dyslexic learners lack intelligence, most have average to above-average intelligence. Comprehension is not the problem – comprehending by reading is the problem.

Many dyslexics learn better (retain more information) when the information is heard rather than seen. This is really a key to educational success on all levels. While dyslexics should be encouraged to comprehend the written word, it should not be the only way or considered to be inherently better than learning by hearing.

Ben Foss, author of *The Dyslexia Empowerment Plan: A Blueprint for Renewing Your Child's Confidence and Love of Learning*, calls this ear reading as opposed to eye reading. If the desired result is understanding, what difference does it make if the student learned the information by seeing or hearing?

There are many technology tools to help with this. Students should have a few well-chosen technology tools that they are familiar with before heading off to college! Check out Learning Ally (https://www.learningally.org) for access to thousands of audio books including textbooks.

Notetaking

Students should have developed a system for note taking in which they are familiar.

Paper Writing

Students should have experience and confidence implementing steps for writing a 10-page paper with more than two sources. If you are homeschooling, teaching college-level writing skills can be difficult to do.

I highly recommend an online writing course called Fortuigence: Essay Rock Star (http://www.fortuigence.com). Taking a composition class through a homeschool group or co-op can provide excellent opportunities for practice in writing.

Whatever you choose, find a way for your students to practice, practice, practice their writing skills.

Test-taking Skills
Students should have developed a system for preparing for tests and exams,
strategies for analyzing multiple choice questions and methods of reducing test-taking anxiety.

Study Skills
Students should learn good study habits as well as finding a study group. They should be aware of the dangers of waiting to the last minute and 'cramming'.

Memory Strategies
Students should learn memory strategies that are the most effective for their unique learning style. For

example, one of our kids loves the Quizlet app for studying because he needs the auditory options that Quilt provides. Another one of my kids prefers to write out her flash cards. The act of writing information is more helpful for her to remember.

Organizational Skills

This is often referred to as Executive Function by researchers. Dyslexics tend to be more right-brained and big-picture oriented. This is an excellent skill for designing and engineering but not so helpful when you are trying to find your notes or syllabus or even your entire notebook! Dyslexics need to be taught some key organizational skills:

- Develop a system for keeping track of materials such as projects, books and papers.
- Know how to read and follow a syllabus and to work with due dates.
- Utilize a calendar – Google calendar is an excellent tool that can be synched with a smart phone to your computer.
- Develop a system for scheduling and managing time.

- Be able to prioritize study time over social time.
- Have a method for coping with boring tasks like breaking big projects down into chunks or steps.
- Use technology effectively.

Time Management Skills

In a study conducted by the Davidson Institute for Talent Development on successful students with dyslexia, time management strategies were the number one most helpful compensation method these students possessed. Students were taught to organize their time using one-month organizers, semester overview calendars and were taught to analyze each week and sometimes each day to maximize their time. Time management skills grew over time as the students learned what worked and what didn't.

Tips for successful time management:

- Set a daily time for review of each subject. Begin with the most difficult or boring subject.

- Allow more time than you think it will take and keep track of how long a particular task takes.
- Chunking: breaking assignments down into chunks and assigning days (and marking them on a planner or calendar) for completion.
- Consider taking more than 4-years to complete college.
- If you must work to earn money, try to make it related to your major.

Self-Understanding or Metacognition

This self-understanding is often referred to as metacognition. Once your dyslexic student enters the college campus, they are responsible for their education. No one is going to call mom if an assignment is missing or if it is being done poorly. Helping dyslexic students to understand their dyslexia and to be able to converse easily about it with professors and other campus personnel is a key to their success.

Metacognition skills your student should have are:

- Being able to define and describe their learning style and diagnosis (if they have one).
- Have a good understanding of their educational test results. They can meet with the tester or tutor to better understand this.
- Know their academic strengths and weaknesses.
- Know which academic supports they need to be successful.

By law, all colleges offer support at varying levels. We'll talk more about that in Chapter # Types of College Support Programs. This self-understanding will help when it comes to choosing the type of college and major area of study. Once your child hits the college campus he or she will be responsible for his or her own education and being able to understand themselves, how they learn best and what accommodations they need is a key to their success.

Self-Advocacy

Because college students are adults, they cannot be compelled to use services or accommodations – neither will they likely be offered. Dyslexic students need to be able to know what they need and be able to advocate (ask for and find help) for themselves.

This means that your student must:

- begin to understand his or her legal rights
- know when and how to ask for help
- be able to schedule their own appointments with doctors, advisors and counselors
- investigate and utilize available resources

Self-advocacy relates to a student's self-awareness. Our kids need guidance to understand their strengths and weaknesses in order to choose appropriate strategies and advocate for academic accommodations. They should be able to communicate this clearly to their teachers/professors and faculty. Developing a rapport with professors was key to getting the help and accommodations needed.

Accommodations include:

- Extra time on tests
- Alternative testing environments
- Extensions for assignments
- Compensatory Supports
- Students reported that mastering several technological tools aided them in their studies.
- computers
- tape recorders or other recording devices
- spell checkers
- audio books

Again, many colleges have resources for students with learning differences. Help them to find these resources and get plugged in.

Three Factors of Success

The three major influencers of these successful college students are areas that we can work on at home as we prepare our kids for their future, whether or not they choose to go to college.

Self-awareness

Each person developed an understanding of the unique nature of his or her disability, personal style and preferences and the most appropriate or effective compensation strategies. This includes choosing a major that is a good fit with these personal strengths.

Dedication

Each student applied an extraordinary amount of time and effort to their studies.

Self-confidence

Each student had a high degree of comfort with using compensation and accommodations.

The Importance of Motivation and Confidence on College Success

It has been shown that the key determiner of college success is not necessarily academic ability, rather determination and grit.

Does your child have an academic subject that he or she finds interesting?

Do they know what they want to get out of their college experience?

Are they excited about college?

Can they imagine their lives in 10 years? Do thy have a vision for their future and what role college plays in that?

It is important for any college student, much less the dyslexic ones, to be able to clearly visualize their success. If they are motivated to complete college, they will be less likely to give up or skip classes and exams.

The Importance of the Early Educational Experience

Many of the students in the study felt that during their early school experience, their learning struggles were viewed by their teachers as synonymous with below-average ability. They reported that the typical strategy in their classroom was to make the coursework easier rather than instructing them in compensation strategies. They also stated that their early educational experience had strongly influenced their attitudes towards themselves and their ability to compensate for their weaknesses. Many of their school experiences were very negative.

A Note About the Foreign Language Requirement

Students who have trouble with oral or written language in their mother tongue tend to have difficulties learning another language. With the right types of instruction (systematic, structured, multi-sensory) and accommodations for the student's individual learning style, they can learn another language. As with learning the English language, it takes dedication, perseverance and hard work.

In some high schools, colleges and universities in the United States, students are allowed to substitute a course on culture for the foreign language requirement. Here in California, high school students are allowed to substitute one year of either visual or performing arts or career technical education for the language requirement. Colleges may also be able to authorize substitutions for the foreign language requirement. If your child has a documented learning disability, obtained through testing, contact the admissions officer or the director of the office of services to students with disabilities at the school your child wishes to attend.

Homeschooling Environment

I was so excited as I read this study. It served to solidify my belief that we as parents can work to foster the types of attitudes and behaviors that lead to successful college experiences for our kids. Confidence, independence, self-awareness, and focused attention on time management and study skills. We can do that!

Chapter 9. Technology Helps for the Dyslexic College Student

With the explosive growth in technology available today, dyslexic students have more opportunities than ever before to find work arounds for their areas of academic weakness.

As with study skills and self-advocacy skills, the use of compensatory technology helps should be mastered as much as possible before the first college assignment for a smoother transition.

Technology Tools for Organization and Time Management

We talked yesterday about the skills needed for college success. From word processing programs (with spell checkers) to electronic calendars and organizers, there are many ways to help your dyslexic student become more organized. The following technology tools have been specifically chosen for their particular ease of use and usefulness to people with dyslexia. Have your student get familiar with a few that he or she finds useful.

Google Drive: documents, spreadsheets, forms and presentations

Google Sites: web pages, web binders, group projects

Gmail: powerful email provider through Google

Google Calendar: tasks schedules, daily agenda, alerts, sync to smart phone

Evernote: record, organize notes, folders

Variety of Homework Apps: weekly schedules, keep track of assignments

Technology Tools for Brainstorming and Mapping
The right-brain strengths of the dyslexic learner make them natural inventors and 'idea people'. Help them to find a way to document and organize these creative thoughts in ways that make sense to them by trying one of these visual organizers.

Inspiration

Popplet

Stickies

Brainstorm

Technology Tools for Writing (Speech to Text)

When we first started our dyslexia journey almost 20 years ago, speech-to-text technology (apps and programs that turn your spoken words into text) was like something out of a Science Fiction story. People were talking about this technology but the programs that were offered were expensive and didn't work well. Over the years, the speech to text technology has vastly improved.

Dragon Dictate: Speech to Text – converts speech into text, or try Dragon Naturally Speaking for the desktop.

Technology Tools for Studying

Studying is a part of college that is inescapable. Finding tools to help your student study smarter will go a long way in preparing them for college success.

Quizlet: Flashcard app that also has an audio function that reads the flash cards to your auditory learner.

Text to Speech: There are many of these apps that can read text from a web page, email or even social networking sites and read it to your student.

Kurzweil: Helps with highlighting and outlining text.

Voice Recorder and Voice Memo apps: There are many of these apps that can be used to record notes to yourself or dictate messages and assignments. White Board apps: Educreations, ScreenChomp Visuwords: Graphic dictionary – excellent for visual learners.

Reading and Input (Text-to-Speech)

Since dyslexic students often learn better by hearing, finding ways to use 'ear reading' will help them learn faster. Text-to-speech technology reads text out loud.

Web Reader HD: Text-to-speech app that can read web page content. Super easy to use and mostly effective.

Learning Ally - Excellent resource for audio books, including textbooks

iBooks features – has text to speech function built in.

Most e-readers have built-in text-to-speech capabilities today

Visit the Resources Page at HomeschoolingWithDyslexia.com for more excellent links to useful technologies for the dyslexic student.

Is Using Technology Cheating?

Some people are still under the misunderstanding that using technology to learn is somehow cheating. Everybody learns differently with different strengths and weaknesses. Finding the way that you learn best is common sense. If your student would benefit from using technology in his or her studies, by all means, let them!

Chapter 10 Understanding the Differences Between High School And College

There are some significant differences between high school and college with which you and your students should be familiar. Essentially, students become much more independent in college; they are fully responsible for their assignments, schedules, and obtaining any accommodations they may need.
 Since many students with dyslexia struggle with organization, handling this newfound independence can result in problems.

Important Difference Between High School and College

High School
- Others structure student's time
- Parents and teachers remind, prioritize and guide student
- Spend approximately 6 hours/day, 30 hours a week in class
- Student is told what to study, learn and do
- Teachers remind student of incomplete work
- Effort counts

- Parents get notified

College
- Student manages own time
- Student makes own decisions
- Only 12-16 hours of class/week
- Student is responsible for figuring out what to learn study and do
- Nobody reminds student of incomplete work
- Results count
- Parents are not notified

As you can see from this list, college students need to be self-motivated and have some solid organization and time management skills to manage all of their new found freedoms and responsibilities.

Legal Differences Between High School and College

Another difference between high schools and colleges are that high schools are governed by the Individuals With Disabilities Act (IDEA) but colleges are governed by the Americans with Disabilities Act

(ADA). If you are in a public school and have either an IEP or a 504 Plan, these will be obsolete in college. If you need accommodations in the college classroom, it will be up to you to obtain them.

In fact, it is illegal for colleges to ask about disabilities in the admissions process. It is up to you as to whether you disclose your dyslexia during the application process. You don't have to disclose any learning disabilities to receive special services once you are a student there. Read this interesting article from US News on the benefits of disclosing a learning disability during the college application process.

Modification and Accommodations in College

One of the major differences in college is that students no longer receive modifications to the curriculum as they may have done in high school. College students with dyslexia will be expected to complete the same assignments as everybody else. However, in college, dyslexic students can expect to receive accommodations such as extra time for assignments and tests and course substitutions in subjects like foreign languages.

In order to receive accommodations, you will need to actively report your learning issues and be in communication with the Office of Student Services and your instructors.

Most colleges have an office dedicated to assisting students with disabilities. You are encouraged to contact them even before you apply to see what kinds of services you can expect from that school. You will need to show proof of your dyslexia, usually in the form of a report prepared by a licensed psychologist or doctor that indicates the tests that were used to determine your learning disability and the scores you achieved. I will talk more about accommodations within the college in chapter # Types of College Support Programs and and in chapter # – Understanding the Application Process. For now, know that most colleges offer some level of support.

Understanding the differences between high school and college will help you as you plan for the college years. Teaching your students to be self-aware and how to self-advocate now will help them immensely when they begin to experience the responsibilities and independence of the college campus.

Chapter 11:   Different Types of College Support Programs

We spent the last few chapters learning a lot about what our kids can expect in the college years. There will be challenges for our dyslexic students to be sure. One way to minimize those challenges is to choose a college with the right type of support system for your child with dyslexia.

All colleges are required by the Americans with Disabilities Act to provide accommodations if you have provided documentation of a diagnosed learning disability to the support services office of the school. Accommodations provided are extended time on tests, a quiet room for test taking, note takers or the use of a computer. Some colleges will even provide alternative forms of testing (i.e. oral), use of a calculator, tape recorder or other assistive technologies.

While all colleges are required to provide a minimum level of support, some colleges provide more. Let's look at the different levels of support that can be found on college campuses.

Comprehensive Structured Programs

This type of program has the highest level of support. It usually involves an extra fee and a separate application.

Services that may be included are:

- staff trained in learning disabilities
- special orientation programs
- curriculum modifications
- assistance with advocacy and accommodations
- weekly academic monitoring and counseling

Colleges with Comprehensive Structured Programs:

American University
Curry College
University of Arizona
University of Denver
American International College
Marist

Coordinated Services

This type of program provides students with moderate levels of support. They generally have learning disability specialists that assist students. In our state of California, all of the state universities have this type of program.

Services that may be included are:

- learning strategy instruction
- counseling
- tutoring (often peer tutoring)
- assistance with advocacy

For an extensive list of colleges that are dyslexia-friendly, visit, www.college-scholarships.com/learning_disabilities.htm.

Basic Service Programs

This type of program provides the minimum amount of support necessary in order to comply with the law.

Services that may be included are:

- extended time
- quiet room for testing
- note-takers
- use of computer

Colleges Specifically for Students With Learning Difficulties

Beacon College
Beacon College is accredited college in Leesburg, Florida that offers traditional classes and curriculums, but they design each class in a way where dyslexic

students learn and excel. Beacon College offers both Associates Degrees and Bachelors Degrees.

Landmark College

Landmark College in Putney, Vermont is also an accredited college that offers various Associate Degrees. Landmark takes the approach of teaching students the skills and strategies necessary for success in college and the workforce.

It is recommended that families visit potential colleges and speak directly to their department of student services to determine exactly which types of support their students can expect to receive.

Chapter 12: How to Find the Right College for Your Dyslexic Child

Finding the right college for a student with dyslexia can make a huge difference in his or her level of confidence and success.One way to begin the search for just the right college is to begin by choosing colleges you would like to attend. Then head over to the college website and search for 'student services' or 'disabilities' to find what services are offered. If you can call and speak to the person who or department which is responsible to arrange the accommodations, here are some questions to ask:

- What types of academic accommodations are typically provided to students with learning challenges on your campus? Will this college provide the specific accommodations that I need?
- What types of support are available?
- Does the program have professional tutors or peer (student) tutors? Does the college have tutors available who are trained and

understand the needs of students with learning differences?

- Are students assigned a regular appointment or do they receive services on a drop-in basis?
- Are there additional fees to participate in the support program?
- How long has the support program been in place at this college?
- How many students are enrolled in the support program?
- What is the retention rate of students with learning challenges at this college?
- How many students with learning challenges have graduated in the past 5 years? What were their major fields of study?
- Is there a summer pre-college program available to incoming first year students?

Resources for Finding a College for Your Student with Learning Disabilities

CollegeBoard.com is a great way to seek for colleges that match your student. Go to College Search, and fill out the survey, marking that learning disabilities services are needed.

For More Information/Resources

If you have been educating and advocating for your dyslexic child for long, you know the importance of getting educated. Preparing for college is no different. The following list of books are gold mines of information to help you and your child find the right college and get the help that they need.

The K&W Guide to College Programs & Srevices for Students with Learning Disabilities or Attention Deficit/Hyperactivity Disorder

Colleges That Change Lives: 40 Schools That Will Change the Way You Think About Colleges

Preparing Students With Disabilities for College Success: A Practical Guide for Transition

Survival Guide for College Students with ADHD or LD

Learning Outside the Lines: Two Ivy League
Students with Learning Disabilities and ADHD Give
You the Tools for Academic Success and Educational
Revolution

Chapter 13: Options for After High School

Not all kids want or need to go straight to a 4-year university after high school. There are many options available. If you have a child nearing high school graduation, it is important to know what viable options are out there for their foray into the adult world and help them to choose the best fit for your unique child.

Dyslexic learners have been attending and graduating from college for as long as college has been around. With the right skills, accommodations and campus support college is all the more doable for the dyslexic student. Take a lesson from your dyslexic learners who are prone to think outside the box and don't be afraid to think outside the box when you are choosing from the many options available for pursuing education after high school.

Most people think of going straight to a four-year university right out of high school as the best option for their kids, but there are actually many options.

The best choice for your student is unique to your family situation.

Post Grad Year

A post grad year should not be confused with a Gap Year which will be covered next. A Post Grad year refers to an extra year of high school that is generally taken at a freestanding boarding school. The purpose of a Post Grad Year is to give students time to improve academically or emotionally. If your child is enrolled in a public or private school, they will have earned their high school diploma before taking their Post Grad studies.

For homeschoolers this may involve working with your homeschool group to rearrange credits allowing for essentially a fifth year of high school. This entails pushing back 9th grade credits onto the 8th grade year and proceeding with another year of high school.

This growing trend has the benefit of giving your student more time to prepare for the SAT or ACT, time to mature and time to practice more of the skills needed for the transition from high school to college.

Gap Year

A Gap Year is when a student applies to college but defers attendance for one year. Usually this time is used to explore interests or gain meaningful work experience.

There are actually Gap Year programs that are designed with this type of student in mind. These programs provide different opportunities for travel and service for the student who wants time to expand their perspective and gain direction that may give the college years more meaning and focus.

Community College

Community colleges may be the right route for your student. Benefits to choosing a Community College straight out of high school (or even after a Gap or Post Grad year) are:

- There is no SAT or ACT test requirement. This should not be your main reason for choosing the Community College. There are accommodations available for students with dyslexia and more and more colleges will waive the SAT requirement for these students as well. We'll talk more about how to get accommodations on college entrance exams tomorrow.

- Provides time for remediation if needed. Community college students can take remedial level courses in math and english if needed while at the same time getting used to the changes and new responsibilities of being a college student.

- Schedules tend to be more flexible with more classes being offered in the evenings.

- Cost of tuition is considerably less which can alleviate pressure to graduate quickly. This allows time to take a lighter course load and to switch majors if your student is not quite sure in which direction he or she is headed.

- Many community colleges have partnered with local universities to make transferring straight forward.

Colleges Exclusively for Students With Learning Disabilities

All colleges are required by law to provide some level of support for students with documented (recent psycho-educational testing) learning struggles. These services are provided by the Office of Student Services. We talked more about the different types of college support programs in the last chapter. There are a few colleges that are specifically set up for the student with dyslexia. These colleges provide the highest level of support for dyslexic students than other colleges.

Beacon College

Beacon College is accredited college in Leesburg, Florida that offers traditional classes and curriculums, but they design each class in a way where dyslexic students learn and excel. Beacon College offers both Associates Degrees and Bachelors Degrees.

Landmark College

Landmark College in Putney, Vermont is also an accredited college that offers various Associate Degrees. Landmark takes the approach of teaching students the skills and strategies necessary for success in college and the workforce.

This list is full of links to regular Colleges with with Programs for Learning Disabled Students.
www.college-scholarships.com/
learning_disabilities.htm
While these colleges are not devoted entirely to students with learning disabilities, they do offer programs designed to support students with learning disabilities.

Four-Year College or University

The traditional route for many high school graduates is to go straight to a 4-year University. As I said before, all colleges are required to provide some level of support for students with disabilities. Last week we looked at the skills needed for college success, the types of college support programs available and how to find the right college.

Alternatives to College

With the growing concern over the lack of jobs available to recent college grads and the shocking statistics of crippling college loan debt, wise parents will consider alternatives to a traditional 4-year (or more) college degree. Chapter # is specifically on alternatives to college, but for now, here are four ideas to get you thinking:

Certification

Certification programs are available through community colleges, free standing for-profit schools or corporate programs. These programs vary in price and length of study but they all offer specific training to do a specific job such as medical assistant, information technology, photography, film and many other fields.

Associates Degrees

More and more employers are looking for this 2-year degree often offered by the local community college.

On average, people with an associate degree earn 24% more than those with a high school diploma alone. These degrees usually result in a career-oriented skill such as nursing, or business and information technology.

Trade School

Trade schools allow students to learn basic, professional skills in two years or less. Trade schools eliminate the general-ed type of courses and get right to the core skills needed to get a job.

Start a Business

Not all business owners have a college degree, in fact, many people who don't necessarily make a good traditional student also make some of the best entrepreneurs because of their passion and people skills – two of the most important things to have in a successful business.

Chapter 14:
How to Get Your Student With Dyslexia
Accommodations on College Entry Exams

One major roadblock for dyslexic students trying to get into college is performing well on college entrance exams – either the SAT or the ACT. Low scores on these tests may not accurately reflect a dyslexic students abilities. Obtaining accommodations on college entry exams can help kids with learning disabilities perform at their real intellectual ability.

Dyslexia advocate, Sally Shaywitz, has been working with colleges across the country to look beyond these scores and so you will find more and more colleges who will overlook a poor score in light of your overall high school portfolio.

Test-Optional Colleges

As previously mentioned in Chapter 13, Options for After High School, community colleges do not require SAT or ACT testing and are a viable way to start your student's college years. After completing 2 years, students can transfer into a 4-year university.

Some colleges exempt students who meet grade-point average or class rank criteria while others require SAT or ACT scores but use them only for placement purposes or to conduct research studies. Check with the school's admissions office to learn more about specific admissions requirements.

There are more and more Test Optional Colleges. For a list of schools that do not use SAT or ACT Scores for admitting students into bachelors degree programs, visit http://fairtest.org/university/optional This is not a comprehensive list. You are encouraged to contact any college that your child may be interested in and ask for that school's specific policy regarding college entrance testing.

How to get Accommodations on the SAT

If your dyslexic student is planning on taking the SAT, accommodations are available.

It is important to allow plenty of time to apply for accommodations. The College Board says requests can take approximately 7 weeks to process. They also recommend starting the application process in your freshman year. Students can use any accommodations awarded throughout their high school careers.

Documentation

Eligibility is determined by a review of your student's documentation. Documentation requirements include psycho-educational reports (testing) describing the functional limitations of the disability. For a complete list of which tests are accepted for this documentation requirement, visit https://www.collegeboard.org/students-with-disabilities/documentation-guidelines/learning-disorders.

Functional Limitations

Having a disability does not automatically entitle your student to accommodations. There must also be proof that the disability requires accommodations. Additional documentation should include proof that your student used accommodations in high school and needed them to succeed. A student's functional limitation must result from his or her disability. It describes how the student's daily functioning is affected, as well as how the student's disability affects his or her ability to take College Board tests. A student's functional limitations should be described in his or her documentation.

For more information on documenting functional limitations, visit https://www.collegeboard.org/students-with-disabilities/documentation-guidelines/disability-documentation

For more information on applying for accommodations on the SAT for your dyslexic student visit the CollegeBoard web site at https://www.collegeboard.org/students-with-disabilities

How to Get Accommodations on the ACT

Accommodations on the ACT test is also available. Students can apply for extended time or special testing which includes things like even more time, or further assistance like marking answers or providing a reader who will read the test to your student.

Visit the ACT web site at http://www.act.org/aap/pdf/ACT-TestAccommodationsChart.pdf for complete instructions on how to apply and what accommodations are currently available.

Chapter 15: Financial Aid and Scholarships for Students With Dyslexia

Your student with dyslexia may be prepared for college and even been accepted into their college of choice, but what about paying for college? There are specific scholarships for students with dyslexia.

It used to be that when I thought of scholarships, I immediately thought only of the straight A students. Let's face it, getting free money isn't easy these days. There are a lot of people with amazing transcripts. What hope does a hard working dyslexic student have? A lot. Keep reading.

Many private scholarships are available that grant money to students based on their particular strengths, interests, disabilities and other characteristics or qualities. The following is a list of scholarships particularly for students with learning disabilities.

First Stop – FAFSA

Federal student aid is one way to cover the cost of college. Your first stop should be filling out the Free Application for Federal Student Aid (FAFSA) https://fafsa.ed.gov. This application allows you to determine your eligibility for Pell Grants, federal student loans, and other student aid. This application can be filled out online.

Pell provides grants, which do not have to be paid back, to students who can demonstrate financial need. Students can qualify for up to a maximum of $5,550 for the 2012–13 school year. Need is determined based on the resources which a (dependent) student's family can contribute to the cost of attending college. An independent student's aid amount is based on their own financial resources.

Maximize Grant Money Before Borrowing

After selecting colleges of interest, find out what kinds of financial aid your college offers and try to work with the school to better suit your needs. It is important to maximize grant aid before you borrow to pay for the cost of college. It is also important to use federal student loan programs before borrowing from private sources. Federal student loan programs often provide better terms and conditions and offer more protections for borrowers who might fall behind on their loan payments after school. Overall think before you borrow with these tips from CollegeBoard.org (https://bigfuture.collegeboard.org/pay-for-college/loans/quick-guide-which-college-loans-are-best).

Grants and scholarships

Books

Financial Aid for the Disabled and Their Families 2012-2014 (insert link or author)
This book identifies funding and financial aid resources for high school kids and older with disabilities on education, career development, training, assistive technology, etc.

Web Sites

CollegeBoard.org
Locate scholarships, loans, internships, and other financial aid programs for college that match your education level, talents, and background. Complete

the profile form, including a place to check for learning disability, and Scholarship Search will find potential opportunities from a database of more than 2,000 undergraduate scholarships, internships, and loan programs.

Center for Scholarship Administration

A list of scholarship programs available to students that are categorized by topics and special interests.

CollegeNET

Allows students to search for scholarships that match their personal profiles and needs.

Council for Exceptional Children

A list of grants, scholarships, and funding links and resources for students.

FastWeb.com

A widely used resource on money for college, financial aid, and more.

GreatSchools

A list of books, web links, and specific scholarships and loans that address financial aid opportunities for students with disabilities.

HEATH Resource Center

In the search bar on the right, enter "Financial Aid" for links to scholarships for students with LD.

Sallie Mae

Information and resources to assist students with the financial aid process.

Scholarships for Students With Learning Disabilities

NCLD's list of scholarship opportunities specifically for students with LD.

Students.gov

State funding information for post-secondary education.

U.S. Department of Education

Financial aid from the U.S. Department of Education, including information about Pell Grants, Stafford Loans, PLUS loans and more.

Buckley Moss Society, Anne and Matt Harbison Award

The P. Buckley Moss Society introduces an annual scholarship to provide incentive for, and recognition to, a graduating high school senior with a learning disability who has made arrangements to go to college. This is a grant of $1,000 made toward the tuition at the recipient's chosen college or university.

Anne Ford Scholarship Established for College-Bound Students With Learning Disabilities

The scholarship is an annual gift of $10,000 to a promising high school senior with learning disabilities who plans to pursue a university degree.

FinAid

This comprehensive financial aid website focuses on post-secondary school funding and lists college scholarships for the persons with a learning disability. There's also some information on ways to pay for private education institutions. One helpful part of this site is their Scam Alert section that lists the most common scholarship scams, including suspicious aid offers. You can also sign up for e-mail lists and discussion groups. All in all, it's a very useful site that's easy to navigate and straightforward in its presentation.

The Foundation Center Cooperating Collections

Located in every state, these free funding information centers in libraries and nonprofit resource centers provide a "core collection" of Foundation Center publications and products.

The Hal Hazelett Scholarship

Two $1,000 scholarships for students with LD, one of which is designated for a student pursuing an education and/or a math degree. One ADD/ADHD scholarship will also be awarded.

Incight Go Getter Scholarship

A renewable $750 award available to high school students with physical, learning, cognitive, hearing, or vision disabilities.

LD Resources Foundation

Awards of assistive technology tools (ex. Kurzweil products, Dragon Naturally Speaking and MacSpeech Dictate, Franklin Dictionary) are available to college students diagnosed with LD and/or ADHD. Students must be enrolled at a college/university with the intention of pursuing an undergraduate degree.

The Lime Connect Fellowship Program

This program is available to a current sophomore at a four-year university in the U.S. The student must have a disability, such as LD. The comprehensive program includes educational workshops, interview preparation, organized mentor programs, and continued support and coaching through the recruitment process via a leadership development program, plus a $1,000 award.

The Marion Huber Learning Through Listening Award

Three $6,000 and three $2,000 awards available to high school seniors with LD who demonstrate leadership skills, scholarship and a high level of service to others; must be a member of Recording for the Blind and Dyslexic (RFB&D).

Rise Scholarship Foundation

A $2,500 scholarship is available for a current high school senior with a documented LD who plans to attend a college or university in the upcoming academic year.

Saralu Belkofer Scholarship

Two $2,000 awards are available to students with LD. Students must be a high school senior or involved in post-secondary education. An additional Internet marketing internship is available, if the student(s) is interested.

Smart Kids with Learning Disabilities Youth Achievement Award

A $1,000 award for a student with LD and/or ADHD who has demonstrated initiative, talent, and determination resulting in a notable accomplishment in any field–including art, music, science, math, athletics or community service.

Theodore R. & Vivian M. Johnson Scholarship Program

Available to students with disabilities with financial needs who enroll in a State University System of Florida institution.

Keep Learning – Don't Give Up

If you do not qualify for many of these scholarships, or are simply looking for more opportunities to get money for college, do not despair. Think beyond your learning struggles: what do you want to study? What activities have you been involved in? Are you or your parents members of any associations or groups? Any of these may lead to a scholarship. Sign up for a free scholarship search engine like Fastweb or Sallie Mae's Scholarship Search to create a profile and search for all scholarships that may apply to you. Learn as much as you can about financial aid—the more knowledgeable you are, the better prepared you will be when college bills arrive.

Chapter 16: Alternatives to a Traditional College Degree

As the mother of 8, seven with dyslexia I researched and wrote these last chapters so that I would have the info that I need to help my dyslexic kids to be successful should they choose to go to college.

Interestingly, while I come from a long line of college-educated folks, my husband is not. In fact, I don't know of one of his family members that has attended college. However, he is one of the most brilliant and insightful people that I know. He has single-handedly supported our family of 10 for all of these years by utilizing his exceptional entrepreneurial skills and solid work ethic. We have traveled extensively with the culmination of this adventurous living being that our two oldest kids took their junior years off of high school to attempt amazing world record setting sailing adventures of their own. (Psst... neither of them has gone to college since then!)

It took many years for me to even begin to believe that there are viable alternatives to a traditional college degree.

I wholeheartedly believe that all dyslexic kids can succeed in college if that is where their passions lie, however there are several interesting alternatives to a college course of study.

Just Google 'alternatives to college' and you will be bombarded with insightful writings on the current state of college education; it's financial burdens, lack of guarantee of securing a job, and the state of debauchery experienced on campus.

Is it really worth going into many tens of thousands of dollars of debt with such a dubious return?

I won't go into all of the pros and cons of whether or not to pursue a college degree here. Suffice to say that there are alternatives to college. These alternatives lead to happy, successful and meaningful lives.

If your child is not passionate about attending college, having a good sense of what he or she wants to actually gain by going to college, perhaps you should consider one of these alternatives:

Certification Programs

Certification programs are available through community colleges, free standing for-profit schools or corporate programs. These programs vary in price and length of study but they all offer specific training to do a specific job such as medical assistant, information technology, photography, film and many other fields. Often taking less than a year to complete, these types of training can equip a person with the skills to get a good job earning far more than their uncertified peers.

Associate Degrees

More and more employers are looking for this 2-year degree often offered by the local community college. On average, people with an associate degree earn 24% more than those with a high school diploma alone. These degrees usually result in a career-oriented skill such as nursing, or business and information technology.

Trade School

Trade schools allow students to learn basic, professional skills in two years or less. Trade schools eliminate the general-ed type of courses and get right to the core skills needed to get a job.

Get Experience

Life experience can help a person to hone in on their potential career interests. Work experience can also look good on a resume. There are other experiences as well. Travel, taking classes (without working towards a major) or volunteering are other areas of experience that can benefit a young person as they try to find their niche in the world.

Start a Business

Not all business owners have a college degree, in fact, many people who don't necessarily make a good traditional student also make some of the best entrepreneurs because of their passion and people skills – two of the most important things to have in a successful business.

When I speak to parents of dyslexic children, I notice that many of us are worried. We're worried about these kids who learn differently and how they will ever 'get a job' or get a degree' and 'be successful'.

Passion and Ability

I am always quick to remind them of something that their dyslexic kids already have – the big picture. What does your child like to do? I mean really like to do? What is your child good at? I mean where are their giftings? Where do their talents lie? In my experience, it is often where these two things intersect – passion and ability – that their future lies.

If this formula leads to college – fine. If not, fine. Just as many dyslexic people have overcome the odds to successfully complete Bachelors, Masters, and Doctoral degrees in many walks of life so have many gifted and talented people NOT gone to college and gone on to live successful and fulfilling lives.

It isn't about telling your kids to aim high or to aim low, it is about finding the path that they were made for, which in the end, with the right skills and motivation will result in success and fulfillment.

Chapter 17: A Note For Parents

Many parents who learn that their child (or as in my case, children) have a learning difference like dyslexia, can become overwhelmed at the implications of the diagnosis. They may remember having difficulty in school, but it wasn't until the 1960s that the term learning disability was first used. Because of the many myths surrounding dyslexia and a fear of being stigmatized by family, friends or teachers parents may not speak up about their child's problems. The truth is that connecting with other parents of struggling learners can be one of the best sources of information on how and where to get help.

For all of the books written on how to help our kids who learn differently, I have yet to see something for the parents of kids who learn differently. Frankly, figuring out your child that learns differently can be hard and the learning curve can stretch you in ways that you never imagined. This brings me to my first point:

Find Fellowship

When I was still fairly new to homeschooling and new in my understanding of dyslexia, our family joined a local homeschooling support group. It is a wonderful organization that offers classes for kids, field trips, clubs and support for moms and dads. Without knowing anyone in the group, I signed up for their annual Women's Christmas Tea. I randomly sat down at a table where two moms were deep in conversation. It turned out that both women had sons my son's age who struggled with reading. We started to share and have been friends ever since! We have watched together as our sons (now grown) went through trials and triumphs, encouraging one another along the way.

Being able to share my experience with others who could relate and encourage me was one of the best things that could ever have happened.

Since then, by being open about our kids' learning struggles (without making them the poster child for dyslexia) has allowed for terrific communication with people that I never would have guessed had learning issues.

Build a Network

We are still members of that support group. A few years ago a Special Needs support group was formed. They arrange speakers once a month and share resources for testing, accommodations, curriculums etc that they have found to be helpful. Sharing the cost and sharing the burden makes the journey easier.

A cord of three strands is not quickly broken.
Ecclesiastes 4:12

Be Realistic

While dyslexic learners have many unique strengths, there will be some areas of weakness that will likely remain. I have yet to enter one of my children into the school Spelling Bee. Spelling is a tough area for the dyslexic learner. Organization is another area that will require many dyslexics to struggle throughout their lives. While college is by all means doable for a dyslexic learner, it may not be the best path for them. By prayer and careful observation of their strengths, weaknesses and passions, your child's path will be revealed. Be open to whatever it is that God has planned for your child and stop comparing them to their left-brained linear friends!

Take a Rest

There are times when things seem like they are falling apart. Maybe your child has hit a wall with reading. Attitudes can deteriorate, for teachers as well as students, habits get sloppy and before you know it there is a lack of peace. Sometimes you just need to step back and enjoy your kids for who they are. No teaching, no pushing, just relaxing and doing something that you all enjoy together. As I type this, our kids are packing and preparing for an afternoon at the beach. We have hit that wall of frustration and irritation, so we are going to explore, laugh, breath deep and enjoy.

Chapter 18: A Note to Teachers

Reading difficulties are the most common cause of academic failure and underachievement. The National Assessment of Educational Progress consistently finds that about 36% of all fourth graders read at a level described as "below basic." Between 15 and 20% of young students demonstrate significant weaknesses with language processes, including but not limited to phonological processing, that are the root cause of dyslexia and related learning difficulties. Of those who are referred to special education services in public schools, approximately 85% are referred because of their problems with language, reading, and/or writing. Informed and effective classroom instruction, especially in the early grades, can prevent and relieve the severity of many of these problems. For those students with dyslexia who need specialized instruction outside of the regular class, appropriate intervention from a specialist can significantly help the dyslexic student overcome the most debilitating symptoms.

Teaching reading effectively, especially to students experiencing difficulty, requires considerable knowledge and skill. Unfortunately, current licensing and professional development practices endorsed by many states are insufficient for the preparation and support of teachers and specialists. According to the International Dyslexia Association, researchers are finding that those with reading specialist and special education licenses often know no more about research-based, effective practices than those with a general education teaching license. Most teachers have not been prepared in sufficient depth to recognize early signs of risk, to prevent reading problems, or to teach students with dyslexia and related learning disabilities successfully.

I don't have the answer to this problem. If you are a teacher and are reading this, that is an excellent first step. There are many web sites with information to help teachers to both understand the dyslexic learner and better accommodate them in the classroom so that they can successfully learn and grow and enjoy their school years. Here are a few to begin with:

A Dyslexic Child in the Classroom: A Guide for
Teachers and Parents
www.dyslexia.com/library/classroom.htm

From One Teacher to Another
dyslexia.yale.edu/1teacher2another.html

Creating a Dyslexia-Friendly Classroom
specialed.about.com/od/managementstrategies/a/
dyslexic-friendly-classroom.htm

Dyslexia: What Teachers Need to Know
www.scholastic.com/teachers/article/dyslexia-what-
teachers-need-know

Working With Dyslexia: Especially for Teachers
www.ncld.org/students-disabilities/ld-education-
teachers/working-dyslexia

Teaching Methods for Dyslexic Children
www.dyslexia-teacher.com/t6.html

Chapter 19: A Note to Students

Did you know researchers have found that self-made millionaires are 4 times more likely to be dyslexic than the rest of the population? Some people say that it is because you have had to figure out different ways of doing things for so long, you are well-trained entrepreneurs!

While the school years can be a difficult time for dyslexic learners, your exceptional gifts and talents have made some of the most successful people in the world - outside the classroom. So while some people, at some times, may look at dyslexia as a disability, it really is a learning difference that is accompanied by some impressive strengths.

Dyslexic Strengths
- Often highly creative
- Persistent
- Can easily grasp new concepts
- See patterns, connections and similarities that others don't see
- Excellent at solving puzzles

- Holistic: they see the big picture, don't get lost in details, get to the important aspects
- Excellent comprehension of stories read or told to them
- Strong reasoning skills
- Understand abstract ideas
- Inclination to think outside the box

Dyslexic Careers

These strengths lend themselves nicely into these careers:

- Science/Research
- Marketing/Sales
- Design
- Woodworking/Carpentry
- Artist
- Actor
- Architect
- Mechanic
- Engineering
- Photography
- Music
- Athletics
- Software design

For inspiration head over to this web site for an impressive list of famous dyslexics www.dys-add.com/symptoms.html%2523famous.

Don't give up. You have gifts and talents that are uniquely yours. You may have to think outside the box some to find them, but that is okay! Thinking outside the box is a natural talent of the dyslexic mind.

APPENDIX A: RESOURCES

Best Books on Dyslexia

There are many well-written books on the subject of learning differences. The books I have listed here are books that I own and have read and reread.

Right Brained Children in a Left Brained World by Jeffery Freed and Laurie Parsons

Written by a former teacher and educational therapist, this book explains the unique differences that predominantly right-brained thinkers possess. Contains a checklist to determine whether you and your child are right-brained thinkers and a simple step-by-step program to help these kids learn and excel utilizing their unique strengths.

Overcoming Dyslexia by Sally Shaywitz

When this book came out in 2005, it turned the world of understanding dyslexia upside down. Written by neuroscientist Dr. Sally Shaywitz of Yale University, it chronicles the ground-breaking research using the results from Functional MRIs to trace the cause of dyslexia to a weakness in the language system at the phonological level. Don't let the terminology scare you. This book is written for the lay person and is a treasure of information well-grounded in science. Includes exercises and techniques for working effectively with your dyslexic child.

Homeschooling the Challenging Child by Christine Field

Written by a former lawyer turned homeschool mother. Chapters address how to deal with issues stemming from various learning disabilities, attention disorders, personality clashes, learning styles, discipline problems, managing stress and discouragement, how to plan a program, and the importance of keeping in mind the tenets of God's love and forgiveness. Hands-on tips for managing a successful home education program, as well as how to find professional help from support groups.

Unicorns Are Real: A Right-Brained Approach to Learning by Barbara Meister Vitale

Don't let the title of this book put you off. "Unicorns are real" was a statement made by a young student of the author that was the catalyst for leading her to begin to better understand the differences between her right-brained students and left-brained students. Written in an easy to understand style and full of real life practical strategies for teaching the predominantly right-brained learner. The book begins with an easily understood, yet surprisingly in-depth description of brain structure and function as it pertains to learning. The book also contains simple, do-at-home procedures for testing your child for brain dominance.

Your Child's Growing Mind by Dr. Jane Healy
Considered the classic guide to understanding children's mental development. She explains the building blocks of reading, writing, spelling, and mathematics and shows how to help kids of all ages develop motivation, attention, critical thinking, and problem-solving skills. She also looks at learning issues, ADHD, and the influences of electronic media – all through the lens of the science of childhood development.

Brain-Integration Therapy Manual by Dianne Craft

Brain Integration Therapy is a method to enhance brain function are by performing simple physical movements that cross the midline. It has been found to profoundly improve ADD/ADHD/Dyslexic conditions as well as other learning struggles. In a few minutes a day, you can vastly improve your child's focus, reduce stress and improve school performance. Yes, this works!

Parenting the Struggling Reader by Susan Hall and Dr. Louis Moats

A very comprehensive, practical guide for recognizing, diagnosing and overcoming any childhood reading difficulty. Written by a mother of a struggling reader (who is also on the board of directors of the International Dyslexia Association) and an educational researcher, this book contains both the clinical information a parent needs but also the practical, everyday solutions and tips needed to successfully help your struggling reader.

Contains an extensive explanation of our role as advocate for our children. Sections are as follows: Identify

Testing

Accurate diagnosis

Determining what instructional approach will be most effective for your child

The Dyslexic Advantage by Brock Eide and Fernette Eide

With inspiring testimonials, this paradigm-shifting book proves that dyslexia doesn't have to be a detriment, but can often become an asset for success. The struggles as parents of struggling readers are often immense as we work to advocate for them in a society that, more often than not, discards a dyslexic intellect as inferior and unlikely to succeed in life. This wonderful book explains through example after example how the complete opposite is the case. Dyslexic minds may have troubles with conventional ways of "doing things" but it is for that reason that they have been the pivotal forces behind discoveries and innovations that have led our culture forward for centuries. Includes extensive coverage of accommodations (like speech-to-text software and digital books).

Homeschooling Children with Special Needs - Turning Challenges into Opportunities by Sharon Hensley

Another excellent guide to the realities and methods, including lots of curriculum suggestions, for homeschooling any child with special needs.

Best Web Sites for Dyslexia: For Parents

Get Ready to Read A wealth of information and tools to educate parents on how younger kids (ages 3-5) learn, the stages of reading readiness and tips, webinars and links to more excellent resources than I can name here. Includes a free online screening tool that you can do with your emergent reader right at home to asses the skills of your child. The screening results let a parent know whether or not to take specific actions such as introducing new skills, offer additional instruction, practice or support or if further assessment is needed.

LD Online One of the best informational sites on learning disabilities and ADHD. The site features hundreds of helpful articles, multimedia, a comprehensive resource guide, discussion forums, and a referral directory of professionals, schools and products. Also offers information and resources for the transition from high school to college and from college to the workplace for adults with learning disabilities.

Dyslexic Advantage From the writers of the book of the same name. This site is full of information, current research and forums to start and contribute to discussions of issues important to you.

The Yale Center for Dyslexia & Creativity Concise site full of information for parents, educators and policy-makers.

Wrightslaw Special Education Law and Advocacy The leading website about special education law and advocacy, with thousands of articles, cases and free resources.

Bright Solutions for Dyslexia Susan Barton is the developer of the Barton Reading & Spelling System. This is a science-based program that you can easily do from home. Be sure to have your child tested before beginning any treatment program to know for sure what your child's specific areas of weakness are. Her site is full of information on everything from defining dyslexia to finding a tester or tutor in your area.

Great Schools An excellent resource for articles on all aspects of handling dyslexia, both for homeschool and public school. Used to be SchwabLearning.

Yahoo! Groups_ Many different online groups for parents of dyslexic children.

From Emotions to Advocacy: The Special Education Survival Guide A treasure of resources for learning effective advocacy skills within the public school. Excellent!

Best Computerized Reading Instruction for the Younger Struggling Reader

Starfall A free public service to teach kids to read with phonics. Starfall combines phonemic awareness practice with a systematic phonics instruction and highly engaging visuals. My kids love this program. Check out the Starfall iPad app too.

Reading Eggs For children from 4-7 who are learning to read. Focuses on a core reading curriculum of phonics and sight words using skills and strategies essential for sustained reading success. Free 14-day trial and then costs about $10/month.

Reading Horizons Discovery at Home Reading Horizons Discovery at Home is an explicit, systematic, research-based phonics program for grades 1-3 based on the Reading Horizons method. Comes in both Direct Instruction physical materials and/or an online version. Reading Horizons offers tons of teacher helps including webinars, games, worksheets and a blog.

Best Computerized Reading Instruction For the Older Struggling Reader

Reading Horizons Elevate Reading Software: Older struggling readers have the same problems as younger readers and need to learn and master the same skills. The key is to find a program that is not 'babyish' and that systematically teaches at an intense enough pace to keep progress steady thus motivating the student. Reading Horizons is all of these things.

Best Blogs on Dyslexia

Dyslexic Advantage From the writers of The Dyslexic Advantage book, their blog is full of news and current topics about dyslexia. Focus on successful dyslexics and how they 'made it'.

Solutions for Struggling Readers Written by educational therapist Carleen Paul, this blog is full of practical, do-it-yourself activities to help your struggling reader.

Help for Struggling Readers Parent and educator, Joan Brennan, has lots of ideas for parents and teachers of struggling readers.

HomeschoolingWithDyslexia.com This is my web site created to help homeschool parents teach their dyslexic kids at home. Contains lots of useful information for all families with dyslexia.

Best iPad Apps for Dyslexia

Web Reader HD Text-to-speech app that can read web page content. Super easy to use and mostly effective.

Dragon Go! (FREE) Allows you to speak what you are searching for on the web so Google, Wikipedia and YouTube are defaults.

Dragon Dictation (FREE) This is a voice recognition app that allows the user to see the text generated through speaking instead of typing. Can be used with some popular social networking sites.

Soundnote ($4.99) A note-taking app that basically turns your iPad into a Livescribe pen. (See above under Compensation Tech) Records lectures and then syncs the audio to what you type or scribble in. The audio recording is time-locked to your typing and drawing. You may want to use a keyboard or stylus for this app to be more functional.

PaperDesk ($2.99) Another note-taking app like Soundnote but that has more options like inserting photos, importing pdfs, organizing pages into notebooks, and an option to export. More complicated to use than Soundnote.

Speller (FREE) Allows you to type in a word phonetically (based on how it sounds) and it will come up with the actual spelling of the word. It also provides definitions to help you understand the meaning of the word.

Reading Trainer ($1.99) Helps improve reading speed with fun exercises.

Read Say ($1.99) Teaches grade appropriate Dolch sight words (the 220 words that appear most frequently in reading) by showing each word, speaking it aloud and tracking your progress. We LOVE flashcard apps!

Sound Literacy ($24.99) Open-ended design for teaching phonemic awareness, phonological processing, and more sound awareness activities - all weaknesses in struggling readers. App features phoneme tiles for hands-on manipulating. See their web site to see if this is a good fit for your family www.soundliteracy.com

Idea Sketch (FREE) lets you draw a diagram (mind map, concept map, or flow chart) convert it to a text outline and vice versa/ It can be used to brainstorm ideas, illustrate concepts, make lists and outlines, and more. Great for visual thinkers.

Best Compensation Technology for Dyslexics
Livescribe Smartpen
An amazing device, this is a pen that captures everything you hear and write while linking your audio recordings to your notes. Great for a student sitting in a lecture hall. Later, playback the recording or tap your notes with the pen to go back to just one

particular area. Our daughter used this in her first college classes and loved it.

Dragon NaturallySpeaking

This is a speech-recognition computer program that can be used to, among other things, dictate everything from answers to schoolwork, to a five-paragraph essay. You can even dictate emails, surf the web with voice commands or dictate on your smartphone.

Best Sources for Audiobooks

Books Should Be Free Free public domain audio books and ebooks for use with iPhone, Kindle and mp3 players.

Spreadsong Free audiobooks from iTunes

Bookshare An online library of digital books for people with print disabilities. It operates under exception to US Copyright law which allows copyrighted digital books (not just public domain) to be made available to people with qualifying disabilities. To become a member you must prove that you have a need for their service by completing a proof of disability form (available on their web site).

Learning Ally A non-profit group that provides audiobooks and textbooks to students with learning disabilities and visual impairments. Used to be called Recordings for the Blind and Dyslexic.

Best Source for Educational Resources

Educators Publishing Service An impressive array of curriculum for all subjects with a special section for Learning Differences that is excellent. Lots of free resources for parents and teachers as well.

Best Educational Therapy/Dyslexia Treatment Program

National Institute for Learning Development Many treatment/tutoring services for the struggling reader are focused on teaching systematic phonics instruction. There is nothing necessarily wrong with this approach. However, a program that enhances and strengthens the struggling reader's weak auditory and visual memory and other specific weaknesses (determined by accurate testing) improve in their reading ability much faster. Check out NILD.org for more information and to find a tutor near you.

Lindamood Bell Highly trained tutors use an Orton-Gillingham method to help children and adults improve their language processing. This sequential system of teaching phonemes can be very effective for children struggling to learn to read. For over 25 years Lindamood-Bell has been providing research-based treatments for dyslexia, ADHD, CAPD and ASD.

Best Reading Curriculum (Not Computerized)

All About Reading We began using the All About Reading curriculum this year with our dyslexic kindergartner. Now this is a fun program! While Reading Horizons is intense phonics instruction and practice geared for the older struggling reader, All About Reading is hands on, simultaneously multi-sensory introduction into the written word. Every lesson comes with an engaging phonemic awareness activity that is so fun, my son doesn't know he is learning one of the most foundational skills of reading success. Lessons are completely scripted so there is little prep time for mom. The customer service at All About Learning Press is top notch. Specifically designed for the homeschooled student that struggles with reading. This program has all of the elements of a research-based reading program.

APPENDIX B: OUR STORY

Homeschooling has been a huge part of the past 20 years of my life – literally changing just about every habit and practice that I had developed in the 30+years before I set out on that path. Becoming a stay-at-home mom was the beginning of this journey. I, like many of you, read every book I could get my hands on about raising, feeding and nurturing healthy and happy babies and kids. After several years working as a social worker with Child Protective Services prior to having my own kids, and having seen first hand the sometimes brutal effects of neglect, I happily poured my life out for my children believing that they were a precious gift.

After these years, homeschooling was a natural progression of what had already become a lifestyle of learning together as a family. My {then two} kids were naturally inquisitive and fun to be around. How hard could teaching reading, writing and math be?

Famous last words!

My oldest is certainly one of my brightest and he progressed rapidly through his math and even phonics books. We read lots of 'living' books and had many thought-provoking conversations. We began to see a pattern of deeper understanding of the world, not just who did what and when but intangible {and untestable} things like why and what would you have done if you were in their place.

Trouble learning to read

Then we arrived at the silent – e rule. We sat on the couch as I introduced the rule. He agreeably repeated back the rule and attempted to apply it to his reader. Day after day, we rehearsed that rule and day after day he seemingly forgot. Have you had a conversation like this?   "Why can you not remember this? We have discussed it at least 20 times!" Exasperation and frustration began to be the norm during reading instruction and my husband and I knew that 'something' was not quite right.

Otherwise Intelligent

Our son was eloquent, having spoken in full sentences at 15 months of age. He had a huge vocabulary that stunned the casual observer. He was observant and often commented and questioned about things going on around him that we had assumed a 6-year old would not know or care about. Yet learning those phonics rules was like storing water in a paper bag. We poured the info in and somehow during the following afternoon and evening, the information leaked out.

I began to try to remember how I learned to read. Was it phonics based or whole word? How did the teacher teach that entire classroom to read all at once? I could not remember learning to read. I know I was always considered a good reader and as an adult I had no idea that there were actually people that had difficulty learning to read.

Asking the experts for help

By the time our son was 7, we had reached the end of our own understanding and as there was little improvement, we decided to have him tested by an educational therapist. The tests revealed {as we knew} that our son had an incredible vocabulary {equal with that of a 12 year old} and above average intelligence. However, he also had some weaknesses such as visual-spatial grounding and other terms that we had never heard before. The therapist explained a bit about the phenomenon called dyslexia and our world was changed.

We went online and began to research what the 'experts' had to say. We tried everything from vitamin supplements to colored glasses to exercises crossing the midline. We nearly spent more than my car was worth to put our son through vision therapy but we were planning an extended overseas trip as a family so were unable to commit.

Who are the experts?

Interestingly, while we were traveling, we rented our house out to a family who put their kids into the local public school where our children would have attended had we opted to go that route.

Coincidentally, their daughter, who was our daughters age, was dyslexic. I am certainly not saying that this is the case in all public {or even private} schools, BUT in this case due to a lack of understanding {and training} her daughter was teased by students and ridiculed by a teacher who had no understanding of dyslexia and who thought that she was just a lazy girl. Later on our dyslexia journey, when I would come to doubt my own ability to teach our dyslexic kids, I learned of this experience. In fact, this young lady's journey through the public middle and high schools continued to be vastly different {and inferior} to our kids' experience at home.

Take two...

Meanwhile, our younger daughter was beginning to learn to read. She was rather slow to begin to speak. She could talk, she just didn't. Maybe because her older brother never stopped long enough to give her a chance! We did notice that she was not as good at remembering what she heard. In fact, she appeared at times unable to hear us and would often ask us to repeat what we had just said. This was our introduction to auditory processing issues, another root cause of reading struggles.

Walking by faith

We traveled during the years that our oldest two children would be learning to read in school. In between exploring new lands and meeting different kinds of people and languages, we kept chipping away at the reading skills. We gave them plenty of practice at whatever level they were reading and focused on lots of practical hands on experiences. To pass the time while sailing between ports we would read raucous stories of explorers like James Cook, Amerigo Vespucci, Columbus and since we were in Mexico – the wild and adventurous Hernando Cortes while up in the cockpit of our boat. We knew that our kids were not reading where other kids their ages may have been but they were thriving and there was no other alternative at the time

I have painted a somewhat idyllic picture of our life at sea but there were grave doubts milling through my mind at this time as well. I cried out to the Lord for wisdom, desperately wanting my kids to succeed at school. One thing about traveling by boat to remote places is that there are no cell phones, no Internet (except occasionally in port), not many friends and no {english-speaking} church.

God weighs in

It was at this time that I read through the Bible in a year for the first time. I hadn't gone very far in my reading when I began to border on exasperation. The Bible was supposed to be the Owners Manual, the Handbook for Life, yet what did it say about dyslexia or about what I was to do about that?

That was when I was reading about God telling Moses to go back to Egypt to lead the Israelites out – in the book of Exodus. Then I read it. Moses was appealing to God to rethink His plan to have Moses speak before Pharaoh because he was not good with words. So the Lord said to him, "Who has made man's mouth? Or who makes the mute, the deaf, the seeing, or the blind? Have not I, the Lord?"

I suddenly understood that God made my kids' eyes, and their ears and their mouths and every stitch of their being. God does not make mistakes. The thought revolutionized our thinking process about dyslexia. Whether you homeschool, private school or public school, you can help your dyslexic kids discover their God-given talents and gifts and help them have successful lives in school and out.

Where are they now?

The complete story of homeschooling a houseful of kids with dyslexia is too much information for now, although you can keep up with our latest adventures on my blog - **Abundant Life** (mariannesunderland.com). Now that my oldest two kids are young adults, I can look back and see how their life experiences have woven together to produce two unique and very talented individuals who have learned to persevere through difficulties. The flexibility and freedom of homeschooling allowed them to pursue their passions which has led to both of them attaining world records in the sailing world. Our oldest son, Zac Sunderland, is the youngest American to sail around the world alone and our oldest daughter, Abby Sunderland, is the youngest person ever to sail around Cape Horn alone. She also wrote a book!

APPENDIX C: KEEPING PERSPECTIVE

This is a lot of information. Every child, every family is different. Our methods, curriculums and choices are unique to our own families. Although I have been traveling down this road for some time, I do not have all the answers. However, I know Who does!

The Power of Prayer

Never underestimate the power of prayer. Parenting a child with learning struggles can be tricky and frustrating at times. These frustrations are often a sign that something needs to change, either in the curriculum, teaching method or in our own hearts. Directing your kids to pray and praying over them and their education can prepare them for dealing with the lifetime of struggles that we all face – dyslexic or not. Dyslexics are known for being hard working and perseverant. Our struggles in life are meant to strengthen us and for the dyslexic, they certainly can as well.

Guidance

Learning differences vary wildly – no two kids will struggle in exactly the same way. While getting informed is important, ultimately God is the author of all knowledge. Pray that God would lead you to just the right people, resources and help that your child needs.

Wisdom

All children have been created with gifts and talents particular to them. These talents have come from God! Ask Him for wisdom to know your child's gifts. Often these are not in the traditional school arenas like reading, writing. Many dyslexics are gifted in the arts, acting, music, sports. Thirty-five per cent of entrepreneurs are dyslexic. The dyslexic mind does struggle with linear thinking and the written word but they are masterful at finding connections, seeing the big picture and thinking outside the box. They are natural inventors and entrepreneurs. Discovering your child's gifts and talents can significantly improve his school experience and set them on the path for successful future.

Strength

In my experience with parenting and homeschooling kids that struggle with traditional teaching methods, there were school years when we were 50% finished and I was 100% exhausted. What we were using wasn't working or attitudes of frustration and discouragement set in strong. Really, this can happen regardless of whether your child learns differently or not. God uses our trials to draw us and our children nearer to Him – if we will let them. Lay your worries and frustrations before the Lord and ask Him to give you the strength you need to press on. When we are weak, He is strong.

ABOUT THE AUTHOR

Marianne Sunderland is the creator of HomeschoolingWithDyslexia.com, a site dedicated to educating and encouraging parents to successfully homeschool their children with dyslexia.

Marianne is a veteran homeschool mother with over 20 years of experience teaching her 8 children, 7 of whom are dyslexic. She is also a popular homeschool consultant, speaker, a certified Orton-Gillingham dyslexia tutor and author of *Dyslexia 101: Truths, Myths and What Really Works*, a parent's guide to navigating the world of dyslexia.

Marianne understands how it feels to be completely overwhelmed and frustrated by the load of information (and misinformation) about dyslexia that exists today.

Marianne began her homeschooling career in 1995 out of a desire to give her kids the best education possible. Despite a rich educational experience of travel and individualized teaching, her oldest child, though obviously very bright, struggled mysteriously to crack the code of reading. Educational testing revealed dyslexia.

Thus began Marianne's search for the 'cure' for her son's dyslexia. An educated parent and avid reader, Marianne knew that without a strong foundation in reading skills, her son would struggle in all areas of his life and education.

Years later, that boy with his unique and individualized home education, graduated from high school with honors and holds a world record as the youngest American to sail around the world alone.

"Homeschooling not only works, it is the best option for educating kids who don't learn by traditional methods." Marianne Sunderland

Since those early days of tears and exasperation, Marianne has been successfully homeschooling her children with dyslexia using individualized, multi-sensory and research-based methods. All people with dyslexia can learn to read, write and spell with the right methods!

Marianne is a popular speaker at homeschool groups, private schools, conferences and conventions. Her unique perspective gained by homeschooling her own children with dyslexia has helped her to have both the wisdom and understanding that parents need. For more information, please visit www.homeschoolingwithdyslexia.com.

Get Educated With Our Parent Dyslexia Classes

When I set up my online site, Homeschooling With Dyslexia, I set it up with one clear purpose in mind: To help as many homeschooling families be as successful as possible.

Whether I was coaching parents new to homeschooling kids with dyslexia or helping established homeschool families adjust their teaching methods, my goal was the same – I wanted to make it easier for them than it was for me when I first started out some 19 years ago.

After learning and implementing the research-based methods in our homeschool, I realized that:

- School time was no longer wrought with frustration and tears.
- My kids were really learning and the ideas were finally 'sticking'.
- I felt much more confident as a teacher.
- I had a plan that was working for me that could be taught to others.

Our Parent Dyslexia Classes were created to help you quickly and easily get educated about what dyslexia is and how you can most effectively help your dyslexic children not only learn but truly thrive by providing reliable, research-based information, personal experience, practical applications and invaluable lists of resources to help you on your journey. Visit our web site www.HomeschoolingWithDyslexia.com and click on the Parent Dyslexia Classes tab for more information or to purchase.

Enter discount code 'dyslexia101' for 20% any course or bundle of courses.

Printed in Great Britain
by Amazon